Instructor's Manual to accompany

News Writing and Reporting

The Complete Guide for Today's Journalist

Second Edition

Chip Scanlan

The Poynter Institute

Richard Craig

San José State University

Prepared by Richard Craig

New York   Oxford
OXFORD UNIVERSITY PRESS

Oxford University Press is a department of the University of Oxford.
It furthers the University's objective of excellence in research,
scholarship, and education by publishing worldwide.

Oxford New York
Auckland Cape Town Dar es Salaam Hong Kong Karachi
Kuala Lumpur Madrid Melbourne Mexico City Nairobi
New Delhi Shanghai Taipei Toronto

With offices in
Argentina Austria Brazil Chile Czech Republic France Greece
Guatemala Hungary Italy Japan Poland Portugal Singapore
South Korea Switzerland Thailand Turkey Ukraine Vietnam

For titles covered by Section 112 of the US Higher Education
Opportunity Act, please visit www.oup.com/us/he for the
latest information about pricing and alternate formats.

Published by Oxford University Press
198 Madison Avenue, New York, New York 10016
http://www.oup.com

Oxford is a registered trademark of Oxford University Press

ISBN: 978-0-19-533675-7

CONTENTS

CHAPTER 1
NEWS JUDGMENT

Chapter Summary

Having to work with your students to define news might seem unnecessary. If they've chosen to study journalism, it would stand to reason that they'd have some semblance of news judgment. Yet one of the most common laments of journalism teachers today is that their students lack this trait, and it can be a struggle to get them to recognize the newsworthiness of assignments. In this chapter, the authors aim to help them develop that skill by learning how to identify the elements that make a story worth covering and stressing the importance of knowing the audience for their work.

Discussion Topics

1. Find three to five current news stories to share with your class, preferably ones with disparate topics. Discuss the elements that make each story newsworthy, and ask the group which one(s) interest them the most. Then discuss the audience(s) most likely to be interested in each story and whether each appeals to a mass audience versus a niche audience.

2. Current students often believe the Internet is the only source for information, but they'll need to make use of lots of personal sources if they want to be reporters. Identify different kinds of material that reporters might need—facts and figures common to various institutions and businesses—and discuss the sources they might contact and strategies they might employ to get that information. Be sure to go into depth about public versus private information and how differently reporters must approach gathering one kind of material versus the other.

3. Students often have a general notion of different media audiences, but little understanding of why they might matter to reporters. Introduce the notion of how different media content—not just news—caters to audiences based on gender, income, ideology, ethnicity and other factors. Using entertainment content is sometimes a good point of entry for this because students often understand this more instinctively than news content. Once the subject is raised, however, it's a good idea to also remind students that while demographic groupings of people often tend to like given types of content, it's too easy to assume this is true across the board. This is frequently a good way to introduce cultural and ethnic diversity into the class vocabulary and to immediately endow it with

some complexity so that students don't jump to conclusions about different types of people.

4. As noted in the chapter, most news Web sites allow readers to comment on stories. It stands to reason that more newsworthy stories—those most interesting to a publication's audience—would prompt more reader comments. Sometimes, however, certain story topics draw more attention and commentary from a small passionate group than from the publication's audience as a whole. Find examples of current or recent stories and discuss whether you can gauge the newsworthiness of a story by its comments and how this relates to the notion of different audiences within the full readership of a news outlet.

In-Class Exercises

1. Break the class up into groups of three, and then randomly assign each group an element of newsworthiness (timeliness, proximity, etc.). Have each group come up with three news story ideas relevant to that element, then discuss their choices with the class.

2. Take the class for a 15-minute walk around campus. Before you leave the classroom, stress to them that they are to look for anything going on that might be interesting, unusual or otherwise newsworthy. When you return, ask what they found and discuss their answers, stressing how they might develop their observations into story ideas and who they might approach for more information.

3. As a homework assignment, have students email you links to three news stories that particularly interest them. Stress that they should be honest and that the stories they choose don't have to be "serious" stories. Determine the most popular choices, then introduce them in class. Have students write up the elements of newsworthiness each story contains and what the popularity of the chosen subjects says about them as an audience.

4. The book mentions Walter Lippmann's definition of news as "What protrudes from the ordinary." Break the class into groups and give them 30 minutes to complete the following: Using mainstream news sources (be as specific or general as you like in defining these), have them locate three news stories that "protrude from the ordinary"; identify the specific elements that make them unusual; select one of the three they'd most like to cover; and discuss the angle they would take on the story they've chosen.

Identification Questions

1. Good reporters are often said to have a "_____ for news."

2. A basic human trait—simple _____—often unearths interesting elements in otherwise mundane stories.

3. The act of drawing inferences or conclusions from a body of information is called _____ thinking.

4. News that people need or believe is important, if not vital, to their daily lives is said to be newsworthy because it has _____.

5. Once they've found news, the reporters' job is to find its connections to their _____.

6. A common criticism of television news is summarized in the phrase "if it _____, it leads."

7. Technology helped bring about the so-called _____ style of reporting, replacing partisan politics with factual coverage of government and business affairs.

8. News that scrolls along the bottom of a TV screen is known as a _____.

9. The act of ordinary people using audio, video and other reporting technologies to provide news content for professional news outlets is called _____ journalism.

10. Something that happens in your news outlet's local area is said to be newsworthy because of its _____.

ANSWERS: 1: NOSE; 2: CURIOSITY; 3: CRITICAL; 4: RELEVANCE; 5: AUDIENCE; 6: BLEEDS; 7: OBJECTIVE; 8: CRAWL; 9: CITIZEN; 10: PROXIMITY.

Web Links

- Toward a Definition of News (Poynter Online):
  http://www.poynter.org/content/content_view.asp?id=102182
- What Is News? (*Handbook of Independent Journalism* by Deborah Potter):
  http://www.america.gov/media/pdf/books/journalism.pdf#page=7

- With Information Galore, We Need News Judgment (*Los Angeles Times*): http://articles.latimes.com/2009/oct/02/entertainment/et-onthemedia2
- Duke v. Iraq, an Exercise in News Judgment (*Columbia Journalism Review*) http://www.cjr.org/politics/duke_v_iraq_an_exercise_in_new.php

(Note—if a link no longer works, search the title and source of the article to locate it online.)

CHAPTER 2
THE SIX-STEP PROCESS APPROACH
TO REPORTING AND WRITING

Chapter Summary

A challenge for journalism teachers in the 21st century is that some students, while interested in news and/or writing, are intimidated by aspects of being a reporter. Some are reticent to talk to strangers face to face, while others are daunted by the prospects of going through research, editing or rewriting. Even when students get a chance to meet reporters in their classes, some seem to believe there's some magical power involved in generating story ideas and working them into good stories. This chapter should help you show them that reporting involves a method that can be learned and refined. The "process approach" of reporting, focusing, organizing and rewriting information helps to turn something baffling into a series of manageable steps. In the chapter, the authors also define some important tools for thinking and finding focus, for collecting information, organizing stories and writing drafts.

Discussion Topics

1. Brainstorming for story ideas often takes place in small groups, but it can be done with an entire class of manageable size. Sometime before class, come up with five broad, general topics for news stories in your area of the country. It's up to you how vague you want to be—you can start with "crime," for example, or you can go with "burglary" or "theft" to be more definite. Raise these one at a time as general story topics to the class, and for each one ask them to come up with more specific variations that are relevant to their college, neighborhood or region. For each one, keep soliciting more and more specific responses until you have an idea that would make a good story for your school's news outlets.

2. Select three to five current or recent news stories that are centered on a conflict of some sort—between institutions, individuals, companies etc. Students might read the word "conflict" and understand its definition but not immediately recognize conflicts within stories or assignments. Introduce each story to the group and ask them to identify the central conflict in each one. Then talk about the ways in which the conflict, rather than just the facts and figures of the situation, is the true core of the story. Ask the group whether this tension between parties might lend itself to follow-up stories beyond the one you've featured.

3. Discuss the concept of a reporting plan by using the board or screen at the front of your classroom. Create a two-column table—the left column for questions, the right for sources. Either pick a story topic on your own or have your students choose one. Then ask the class who they believe might be useful sources of information. When you have a reasonably complete list, ask the group for questions relevant to the story, then ask which of the sources they've listed might be able to provide useful answers. Discuss how this might be useful in getting organized before conducting interviews.

4. Sometimes to understand how a process works, it helps to take an example and deconstruct the process. Find a feature article or other story with many quotes and have your students either read it ahead of time or at the beginning of class. Put it on the screen in front of class if you have one available. Before going through the story, ask your students what they think its focus is—if students disagree on this in the beginning, that's fine. Then go through the quotes and discuss how each one serves the perceived focus. If class members differ at the beginning on the main focus of the story, this exercise will often clarify the writer's actual intended focus.

In-Class Exercises

1. Have students engage in freewriting about a topic of your choice. Stress to them that this is a technique used to find story ideas and not an end in itself. Also note that for this exercise, they should not worry about the normal conventions of writing, and that they won't be graded on what they produce with freewriting. Introduce a general topic and tell them to simply spew forth the first things that come to their mind about it. Give them 30 seconds or a minute to come up with whatever immediately comes to mind. Then, rather than having them turn that in, have them take what they've freewritten and use it to come up with story angles and/or questions to be answered about the topic.

2. Have students select the top story from a news site of your choice or theirs. Instruct them to read the story, then answer the chapter's five critical questions about it:

   - *Why does this story matter?*
   - *What's the point of this story?*
   - *Why is this story being told?*
   - *What does this story say about life, about the world, about the times we live in?*
   - *What's the story about in one word?*

3. Direct students to a particular feature-length story, which can be read ahead of time or in the beginning of class. Instruct them to create an outline of the story that lists its central

points or concepts in the order they are presented. Then have them discuss whether the story might work better if the facts were ordered differently and why or why not. Stress that they should be as specific as possible.

4. Select three news stories currently or recently in the news, and distill each into a list of its main facts. On a Web page or handout, assign each list of facts the number 1, 2 or 3. Break the class up into groups of three, and number each student as 1, 2 or 3. (Adjust accordingly if your class doesn't divide evenly into groups of three.) Then have each student spend 5-10 minutes writing up a quick few paragraphs of a story just using fact list 1, 2 or 3 corresponding with the number you've assigned them. When done, have the students put their names on their papers, then hand the papers to the group member on their right and have each one make suggestions about how to improve what they've done. Be sure the original author and the editor include their names on the papers before they're turned in.

Identification Questions

1. Creating a list of everything that comes to mind related to a story topic is called
_____.

2. A story's _____ is its central theme or main message.

3. Journalists have to face their fears through _____, forcing themselves to do the thing they fear.

4. Answering a story's most challenging questions involves _____ thinking.

5. Putting a topic in the center of a page and then surrounding it with related ideas is called
_____.

6. In addition to providing facts, journalists must also give their audiences _____ to help them make sense of the flood of available information.

7. Reporters fight writer's block by _____, writing whatever comes to their minds without regard for spelling, grammar or context.

8. Before conducting interviews, it helps to create a _____, a table you can use to connect questions to sources who may be able to provide answers.

9. Once you've gathered the information for a story, it's time to write a _____, or first version of the story.

10. The final step in writing a story is to _____ it—to verify your facts, tie up loose ends and make sure it is accurate, fair and complete.

ANSWERS: 1: BRAINSTORMING; 2: FOCUS; 3: COUNTERPHOBIA; 4: CRITICAL; 5: MAPPING; 6: MEANING; 7: FREEWRITING; 8: REPORTING PLAN; 9: DRAFT; 10: REVISE.

<u>Web Links</u>

- Rejecting Our First Draft Culture: Strategies for Revision (Poynter Online): http://www.poynter.org/column.asp?id=52&aid=20864
- Finding and Developing Story Ideas (Steve Buttry, TBD.com): http://stevebuttry.wordpress.com/2010/02/16/finding-and-developing-story-ideas/
- Five Ways to Use Mind-Mapping Tools in the Newsroom (PBS): http://www.pbs.org/mediashift/2009/08/five-ways-to-use-mind-mapping-tools-in-the-newsroom222.html
- Cool Tools: 3 Fun Ways to Map Your Story Ideas (Write Livelihood): http://writelivelihood.wordpress.com/2008/08/18/cool-tools-3-fun-ways-to-map-your-story-ideas/
- Five Stages of a Story (Michael Roberts, *Arizona Republic*) http://newstrainers.wordpress.com/2009/10/16/five-stages-of-a-story-part-1/

(Note—if a link no longer works, search the title and source of the article to locate it online.)

CHAPTER 3
THE COACHING WAY:
TAKING CHARGE OF YOUR STORIES

Chapter Summary

Getting young reporters accustomed to the often-severe editing in professional journalism has long been a problem for writing teachers. If anything, it's gotten worse in the digital age when students post unedited writings regularly and often respond to suggested edits to their news stories as if they're personal attacks. Fortunately, the coaching method the authors discussed in this chapter relies on writers to improve their own work. It requires some rethinking of traditional techniques, but it has many advantages once students get used to it. The notion is that as writers learn to identify their own shortcomings over time, they'll improve and require less help. In this chapter, the authors discuss coaching techniques and practices and show students how to work with coaches and to act as coaches themselves.

Discussion Topics

1. Select a detailed major story from a local or national outlet to share with your class. Ask students to go through the story with you and list the different facts and concepts the story provides. Allow them to be as specific as you like—the list of facts can contain 20–25 items or more. When done, work with the students to narrow the list down to its "non-negotiable necessities"—the elements they collectively believe absolutely must be present in a story about this topic. Along the way, be sure to ask why each element that's eliminated is less important than those that remain.

2. Find a news story you've written at some point in your career, preferably something lengthy. Have your students read it quickly at the beginning of class, then put it on the screen at the front of the class if one is available. Go through your story and work with students on learning the coaching process by having them coach you. Most important, have students discuss what works and what needs work in the story. Be sure to steer them into a productive discussion—some of them may be tempted to get carried away with the opportunity to criticize the teacher's writing, but the point is to get them used to making straightforward, constructive suggestions.

3. In your school's online news outlet, find a story that could use some improvement (preferably not one written by one of the students in your class). Copy the story's content, then paste it into your word processor, removing the author's name. Put in on your

classroom's screen at the beginning of class. As detailed in the book, perform a "movie reading" of this story while students watch, adding suggestions in caps. As you go through, solicit students' input and discuss the reasons for your suggestions. If you like, when you've gotten through the story, you can then go back through and actually make changes so that students can see how the finished product would read.

4. Have each student email you one news story he/she has written for another class that isn't his/her best work. Select a few examples, then read each one aloud to the class without identifying the author. As is done in professional newsrooms, read carefully and say all punctuation marks aloud in addition to the words. Before you start, encourage students to listen for anything that sounds wrong—run-on sentences, awkward grammar, poor flow or anything else. Encourage them to ask questions or note problems immediately when they arise—make notes on possible fixes, then continue reading. When finished, discuss how reading the story aloud might have made flaws more obvious.

In-Class Exercises

1. Once students have completed a writing assignment for your class, randomly pair them off and have them coach each other on their work. Make sure both coach and writer have access to the story either on paper or electronically, to be able to go through it at the same time. Also be sure they understand that coaching involves describing reactions to stories rather than prescribing solutions and that it's up to the writer to make any changes. Have the writer rewrite the story after the coaching session, and submit old and new versions of the story.

2. After going over Discussion Topic 2 (previously) in class, have students work on improving a story they've written. Tell them to go through the story critically, noting what works and what doesn't work. In addition to turning in the original and rewritten versions of the story, have them briefly discuss what worked and what didn't about the original version and what was done to fix it.

3. Break the class into groups of two or three. Have each student read another's story aloud, speaking punctuation marks as well as words, and have the author take notes on how the story reads. The author should then rewrite the story and include notes on how hearing it read aloud showed areas where the narrative could be improved.

4. Divide the class into groups of three. Using the check-mark method discussed in the chapter, have students look at other group members' stories and check what works and/or doesn't work. Then have the group go over their marks on each member's stories, noting where reviewers marked the same passages in the stories. The author of each story can

then revise the original story based on the areas where reviewers agreed there were issues.

Identification Questions

1. The ability to identify with another person's point of view and to communicate that understanding is known as _____.

2. Donald M. Murray was one of the pioneers of the _____ method.

3. As newspaper and online journalists begin to work in audio or video, many need training in on-air _____.

4. Coaching involves helping writers improve their habits and techniques, while _____ just corrects mistakes in one story.

5. One noted writing teacher says that writers don't need advice about wording or approaches to writing but rather "_____ of people's minds."

6. A technique used in some newsrooms is to read stories _____, to make it plain when writing could be improved.

7. Working in _____ can help students improve their classmates' stories as well as opening their eyes toward shortcomings in their own work.

8. Generally, the person who knows most about a story is the _____.

9. Two questions that drive revision are "What Works?" and "What _____ _____?"

10. Sometimes it's easier to distill a story into its important elements by _____ than by writing.

ANSWERS: 1: EMPATHY; 2: COACHING; 3: PERFORMANCE; 4: FIXING; 5: MOVIES; 6: ALOUD; 7: GROUPS; 8: REPORTER; 9: DOESN'T WORK; 10: TALKING.

Web Links

- The Coaching Way (Poynter Online):
  http://www.poynter.org/column.asp?id=52&aid=33974
- Do-It-Yourself Story Coaching: An Introduction (Write Livelihood):
  http://writelivelihood.wordpress.com/2009/02/27/do-it-yourself-story-coaching-an-introduction/
- Can This Relationship Be Saved? (*American Journalism Review*):
  http://www.ajr.org/article.asp?id=1575
- Finding pleasure in the challenge of a blank sheet (Final column by Don Murray, *Boston Globe*)
  http://www.boston.com/news/globe/living/articles/2006/12/26/finding_pleasure_in_the_challenge_of_a_blank_sheet/
- SuperVision: The Major Motivator (Poynter Online):
  http://www.poynter.org/column.asp?id=34&aid=144767

(Note—if a link no longer works, search the title and source of the article to locate it online.)

CHAPTER 4
STORYTELLING VERSUS SPEED: DEADLINES IN THE 21ST CENTURY

Chapter Summary

It's hard enough to teach students how to write and report like professional journalists, and getting them to do it well daily on deadline has generally been the toughest test of all. In the age of the Internet, however, it's become even more difficult—with today's 24/7 news cycle, there's seemingly no breathing room for young reporters and editors to get up to speed while maintaining credibility and high standards. In this chapter, the authors discuss the competing elements of storytelling and speed and aim to provide ways for students to learn how to cope and even thrive in this challenging environment.

Discussion Topics

1. Find examples of stories from your student news outlet or local news that show people as characters rather than just sources (as noted in the chapter). Go through them with your students and discuss how the author(s) used different storytelling techniques to develop interviewees from just names into people with whom readers can identify. (You might also consider comparing these examples to sources in hard-news articles.) Discuss the types of stories that are more suited or less suited to this sort of character development.

2. Spend some time looking at local and/or national news outlets and locate a story told very differently by two outlets. If possible, find a divide between a facts-and-figures story and a feature, similar to the Kitty Genovese stories in the chapter. Have students read both, then discuss the differences between the storytelling styles. Go through what they believe to be the strengths and weaknesses of each story, and ask whether the conditions under which the story is reported (turnaround, second day, etc.) might influence the way the story is covered by one outlet versus another.

3. Find one or more feature stories to share with the class that are primarily told through one person's point of view. Have the students read the stories, then discuss how different the narrative might have been if told from the perspective of someone else named in the story. Encourage them to be as specific as possible: Would there need to be different facts gathered? Would different elements of the story likely be more prominent?

4. When a breaking news story occurs in your local area, periodically check a local media Web site's coverage of that story as it is updated. Copy or save the site's stories as they come in until the story is finally complete. Show these iterations to your class and discuss why certain elements were reported first and why others followed when they did. Also discuss the thought processes involved and the likely reasons why certain types of information are more likely available right away. Ideally, you can bring a professional reporter in to talk about this process firsthand.

In-Class Exercises

1. At the end of one class meeting, give your students the following assignment to be completed immediately before the next class. On their way to the next class meeting—or at some other point if they have another class immediately before yours—have them simply walk around campus long enough to observe 10 campus details that might prove useful in stories. At the start of class, have each student write up these observations, then write a sentence for each detailing how and/or why it might be used in a story.

2. This exercise involves students knowing and understanding the definitions of "article" and "story" from early in the chapter. Based on those definitions, have them look at online news sites and find three examples of a story and three examples of an article. Have them identify the elements from within the definitions that make each story fit into that category. Then have them attempt to find other elements that each of the stories has in common and that each of the articles has in common. These can include anything from subject matter to deadline status to story structure or anything else you'd like to highlight.

3. As a practice exercise for deadline writing, do some looking around online and find a major story for which you can put together a chronology. Introduce the basic information about the story to your students, then have them write up a lead and nut graf based on only that information. Every few minutes, stop them and give them a little more information and have them start over and write progressively more of the story.

4. Bring in a guest speaker from any profession to talk to your class. Give the class some basic information about the speaker beforehand, and tell them to treat the visit like a press conference. Have the class interview the speaker for 15–20 minutes. Give students the rest of the period to write a profile about the speaker's visit, using not only the questions asked but the observational skills and storytelling techniques outlined in the chapter.

Identification Questions

1. Writing pieces of a story and submitting them to an editor for assembly into a full story is called reporting by _____.

2. Whereas an article may provide facts and figures about a topic, a _____ is something richer, featuring characters, drama and a sense of place.

3. As a reporter, _____ gives you details that you can use to place readers at the scene of an event.

4. An effective _____ to a story echoes in readers' minds, making them think about elements of the piece long after they've finished reading it.

5. A _____ is a full story compiled by an editor from segments sent in by a reporter.

6. Though sometimes difficult while reporting on deadline, it is important for reporters to continually search for the _____ of a story as they go to provide a connective thread throughout the piece.

7. Though it might seem unduly time consumptive, it's still important for reporters on deadline to write _____ of their stories.

8. It's important for reporters to represent people as _____, as individuals with multiple facets, rather than just names, faces and job titles.

9. Smart reporters know that even on deadline, taking a few moments to _____ a story will save them and their editors time later on.

10. As the example of TV reporter Dan Ashley demonstrates, reporters should be ready to take advantage of whatever _____ they might have on hand when a story breaks.

ANSWERS: 1: ACCRETION; 2: STORY; 3: OBSERVING; 4: ENDING; 5: WRITETHROUGH; 6: FOCUS; 7: DRAFTS; 8: CHARACTERS; 9: ORGANIZE; 10: TECHNOLOGY.

Web Links

- A Deadline Column About Writing on Deadline (Dave Kindred, National Sports Journalism Center): http://sportsjournalism.org/sports-media-news/a-deadline-column-about-writing-on-deadline/
- Newswriting Exercises (About.com): http://journalism.about.com/od/writing/tp/newswritingexercises.htm
- The Changing Newsroom: The Influence of the Web (Journalism.org): http://www.journalism.org/node/11966
- Today's journalism motto: Faster, better, more (AAJA Voices): http://blogs.aaja.org/conventionnews/2009/08/13/today%E2%80%99s-journalism-motto-faster-better-more/

(Note—if a link no longer works, search the title and source of the article to locate it online.)

CHAPTER 5
THE REPORTER'S TOOLBOX

Chapter Summary

Among some journalism instructors technology is a sore point and not just because of students checking Facebook during class. Many journalism teachers came through the business when high tech meant carrying a tape recorder and are uncomfortable with new technologies intruding on their time-tested customs and procedures. The fact is, however, that instructors who ignore news gathering technologies do 21st-century students no favors. When technology allows reporters to file completed stories from the scene of a breaking news event—ones that contain not only text but audio, video and photos—what news organization would hire someone who resisted that? Yet young journalists aren't inherently better reporters just because they know technology—they still need scruples, curiosity, persistence and news judgment. In this chapter, the authors examine the tangible and intangible tools reporters can use to gather information and put together stories.

Discussion Topics

1. On the board or screen at the front of your classroom, create a table with two columns—one labeled "Activity," the other labeled "Tool." Ask the class to name off everything a reporter can do at the scene of a breaking news story to gather information (conduct interviews, observe, take photos, take video etc.), and write these all under "Activity." Then have students name every tool—high-tech or not—that reporters can use in the process of gathering information (pen, paper, camera, recorder, smartphone etc.). Draw lines between the activities and the tools that can be used to complete them. These can overlap, and single tools can often be used for multiple activities. Encourage students to be creative about using tools in unusual ways—for example, a camera can be used to record visual details of a scene for use in descriptions rather than as news photos or video. (Even a laptop with a dead battery can be used as a lap desk.)

2. Before your class meets, do a search to find smartphone apps and/or accessories that might be useful for journalists. Either use an existing Web site listing these items on the screen in your classroom or compile your own list. These can include everything from the obvious (apps for audio and video recording, photography and image editing, word processing) to the practical (Bluetooth keyboard to make typing faster, desktop tripod to reduce blur in video and photos, Bluetooth wireless camera shutter button etc.) to the unexpected (spreadsheet for crunching numbers on the spot). Go through the list, discussing both the pluses and minuses of these items, and of taking all this equipment

with you when covering stories. Also be prepared for students to suggest items they may have seen.

3. A controversy among photojournalists involves toning and cropping photos for publication versus falsifying them and committing a breach of ethics. There is plenty of material on this debate available online, with many examples of photos that have been altered. The usual rule of thumb is that photos should represent the reality of a situation and that toning a photo to make it clearer (and thus show more of a scene) is acceptable. Discuss this with your students, showing examples along the way, and talk about the conflicts that can arise between providing eye-catching visuals and upholding journalistic ethics.

4. Ask your students if there are elements of the job of reporting that bother them. It's common for students who haven't done much reporting to feel that asking questions of strangers involves being pushy or rude or intrusive, or that doing research for stories is somehow creepy and invades privacy. Discuss the notion of the reporter's mindset in terms that students might understand. In particular, discuss the idea that when you go to work on a story, you're essentially playing a role. You're assuming the persona of a reporter because during the period of gathering information, that's what you are. For whatever reason, this often helps—perhaps students raised on computers are more comfortable playing roles than thinking of it as social interaction. Sometimes the metaphor of "putting on my reporter's hat" also works. Essentially, this discussion is an exercise in counterphobia, but it's been especially effective when conducted in the familiar environment of a classroom.

In-Class Exercises

1. Pair off students and have them interview each other for 5–10 minutes using only whatever they brought with them to class. If they've brought a phone or other recording device that will capture audio or video, that's fine; if they've brought a pen and paper, that's fine; if they've brought nothing that will record and nothing to write with, they'll have to do it from memory. When done, have them each write a brief profile of the classmate they've interviewed and email it to you. Send each profile to the student profiled and have that student critique the profile for accuracy.

2. Ask the class to pick an issue that annoys or angers their friends (frequently this involves student fees, parking, the cost of textbooks etc.). Have the students send their friends text messages asking for their opinions on this issue, making sure they say that the answers will be used for a class assignment. Then have the students put together a brief story about this issue based on direct quotes from the responses, *keeping all spelling and*

punctuation from the responses intact. At the end of the story, have them count up every grammar, spelling, punctuation or capitalization error they can find and provide a total of each. Then have them write a paragraph about the pluses and minuses of using this method to gather material for news stories.

3. Bring in a friend or fellow faculty member to act as an interviewee. Have your students number off as 1 or 2. In front of the class, interview your guest and have the students assigned to number 1 take notes by hand while those assigned number 2 type notes into their computer. Pause the interview at a point three to five minutes in, and have the students taking notes by hand switch to taking them on computer and vice versa. Continue the interview for three to five minutes more, then instruct the students to use the remaining class time to write a brief story about the interview. Be sure they include their group numbers so you know what facts were taken down by hand and by computer. At the end, have each student write a brief paragraph describing how they believe typing versus writing by hand affected the accuracy of their information.

4. Find a local news story that is covered by one outlet with a TV report and by another with a text-only report. Have your students look at both and write up an analysis of the strengths and weaknesses of both reports, and discuss whether they're related to the strengths and weaknesses of the media of video and text. Would readers of the text story miss important visuals? Would viewers of the TV report lose some of the details provided by the text story?

Identification Questions

1. A _____ is the reporter's most basic tool.

2. The first type of computer software to make an impact on reporters was _____ software, which allowed them to manipulate blocks of text on the screen.

3. Although the _____ is a great tool for reporters, relying too heavily on it can insulate reporters from the people, places and events they are covering.

4. Above all else, a reporter's goal must be _____ because getting facts wrong erodes the credibility of the news organization.

5. Recording audio with a _____ allows you to easily use interview material in a podcast on your news outlet's Web site.

6. Young reporters sometimes need to work on their _____ because it involves walking up to strangers and asking them questions.

7. Working with _____ can give reporters new points of view on stories, adding a visual component to the facts and figures they normally seek.

8. Computer technology that allows manipulation of _____ has caused serious ethical problems for some journalists and news outlets.

9. Because of the move to online news, journalism programs at some universities require their students to take at least a beginning _____ course before graduation.

10. The reporter's _____, his/her approach to doing the job, is considered a tool they must employ to succeed in their jobs.

ANSWERS: 1: NOTEBOOK; 2: WORD PROCESSING; 3: TELEPHONE (POSSIBLY ALSO INTERNET); 4: ACCURACY; 5: DIGITAL AUDIO RECORDER; 6: ASSERTIVENESS; 7: PHOTOJOURNALISTS; 8: PHOTOS/IMAGES (POSSIBLY ALSO AUDIO); 9: MULTIMEDIA; 10: MINDSET.

Web Links

- Journalism Tools (Journalism.org): http://www.journalism.org/resources/j_tools
- The Journalist's Toolbox (Society of Professional Journalists): http://www.journaliststoolbox.org/
- Tools of the Trade for the Mobile Journalist (Suite101.com): http://newspaper-journalism.suite101.com/article.cfm/tools-of-the-trade-for-the-mobile-journalist
- 5 Essential Tools for the Mobile Journalist (Mashable.com): http://mashable.com/2010/02/01/mobile-journalist-tools/

(Note—if a link no longer works, search the title and source of the article to locate it online.)

CHAPTER 6
INTERVIEWING

Chapter Summary

If there's a single element of reporting that worries students more than any other, it's interviewing. How do you walk up to strangers and ask them questions? How do you get people—tight-lipped cops, jargon-spouting experts, everyday folks who aren't accustomed to being interviewed—to give you useful answers? As an instructor, it's important that you demystify this process to allow your students to make the most of their interviews. In this chapter, the authors outline techniques they can use, discuss situations in which reporters may have to make important choices and provides guidelines for effective and ethical interviewing.

Discussion Topics

1. With no prior discussion, start off this chapter's discussion with a simple question: "Be honest—if you had to interview a celebrity political figure or sports star tomorrow, and you could pick any method for interviewing them, which would you choose? Would you do it face to face, over the phone, by email, by texting, by Skype or what?" Discuss the strengths and weaknesses of each method and situations in which each might be used.

2. Find some examples of stories that contain jargon that the average reader might not understand. You can often find these in your school's news outlet or local outlets, but if necessary you can almost always find them in specialized magazines. Go through the stories with your class and ask them the meanings of certain words. If they're truly industry-specific terms, it's unlikely that students will be familiar with them. Stress that this is something reporters run into regularly—when you interview people from different industries and institutions, they'll frequently use terms common within those organizations but largely unknown outside them. Remind the students that their job as reporters is to translate specialized terminology into something that their audience will understand. Students won't want to admit to interviewees that they don't know what a particular word means, but they need to know that having someone explain the meanings of terms is the polar opposite of a "stupid question."

3. In the Internet age, is it possible to overprepare for an interview? Some reporters have said that if they know too much about an interviewee (or think they do), it can stifle the flow of the conversation or make the reporter lose focus on the specific purpose of the interview. Others believe you can never know too much before talking with someone.

Think about your own position on this, then open it up for discussion among your students. Is it more important to focus on the specific information you want, or do you want a well-rounded base of knowledge to allow you to respond to the unexpected?

4. Many professional journalists reject the idea that an interview is a conversation, but it's sometimes best for students learning the craft to think of interviews as "guided conversations." The interviewer has studied up and wants certain information and guides the conversation in productive directions with certain purposes in mind. Discuss this with students in terms of the goals involved, how to be responsive to answers while still focusing on the questions that need to be answered, and what to do if the interviewee begins to guide the conversation.

In-Class Exercises

1. Choose a celebrity, political figure or sports star for a hypothetical exercise—perhaps someone students might have heard of but not know too well. Tell your students they have 15 minutes to do research and assemble questions to ask this person for a profile. Have them write a minimum of 10 questions whose answers aren't simply facts or figures readily available online. Stress that they should start out by learning a little about this person and his/her background before developing questions. Have them email the questions to you, then discuss the submissions in the next class meeting.

2. Invite a professor from another department to come in and be interviewed by students for a mini-press conference of 10–15 minutes. Tell students in advance that this is going to happen, but don't let them know who they'll be interviewing. Give them 5–10 minutes at the beginning of class to look up information on your guest, and insist that they not look up anything further once you get started. At the end, have them each write a brief profile of your guest and turn it in at the end of class.

3. Have the students in your class each choose a prominent person (someone well-known to other students, faculty or the average person) about whom they believe they know "everything." Have them create a two-column document on paper or in a word processor. On the left have the students list everything they know about this person without consulting any information resources at all. When they're done with that, have them list the things they don't know on the right. At the bottom, have them list the three most important pieces of information they didn't know and why they believe those facts are the most important.

4. Give the students 15 minutes to come up with questions to fulfill the following challenge: You can ask the President of the United States exactly five questions, the answers to which will make up the core of a story you're writing. You'd like the president's answers to be as comprehensive and meaningful as possible and to be able to get as much out of them as you can. For each of the five questions you come up with, briefly explain why this question is important to you and what you hope to get out of it. Stress to the students that they should avoid dwelling on any political differences they have with the current president, and focus on formulating questions that will produce interesting and useful answers.

Identification Questions

1. Be sure to _____ that the background material you find for an interview is legitimate.

2. Arriving at an interview armed with lots of background information on the subject is the best way to avoid asking _____ questions.

3. Whenever possible, try to conduct an interview _____ so you can see how interviewees react to questions and interact with people around them.

4. The best way to assure success as an interviewer is to _____ thoroughly before the interview.

5. Interviewing via _____ allows reporters to respond immediately to a source's comments but doesn't generally allow them to gauge reactions visually.

6. While it does have some uses, interviewing by _____ inhibits reporters' ability to ask follow-up questions.

7. One reporter quoted in the chapter likes to interview people at _____ because of what can be learned about them in that setting.

8. Active _____ involves not only noting what a source says but thinking of how it fits in with your understanding of the topic and using that to devise follow-up questions.

9. If you get permission from the interviewee, recording the audio of an interview allows you to use it as a _____ on your organization's Web site.

10. As a general rule, reporters should only use _____ sources as a last resort because such agreements can carry serious consequences.

ANSWERS: 1: VERIFY; 2: STUPID; 3: FACE-TO-FACE/IN PERSON; 4: PREPARE; 5: TELEPHONE; 6: EMAIL; 7: HOME; 8: LISTENING; 9: PODCAST; 10: ANONYMOUS/UNNAMED.

Web Links

- Getting the Most from Your Interviews (Committee of Concerned Journalists):
  http://www.concernedjournalists.org/getting-most-your-interviews
- Interviewing bibliography (Poynter Institute):
  http://www.poynter.org/content/content_view.asp?id=1190
- Reporting/Interviewing Techniques and Tools (American Press Institute):
  http://www.americanpressinstitute.org/pages/toolbox/reportinginterviewing_techniques_and_tools/reportinginterviewing_techniqu/
- Dart Center for Journalism and Trauma
  http://www.dartcenter.org

(Note—if a link no longer works, search the title and source of the article to locate it online.)

CHAPTER 7
RESEARCH

Chapter Summary

Most teachers know that students tend to dread research when it's done for a term paper yet can't learn enough about their favorite celebrity or sports star. If you can have your young reporters channel their thirst for knowledge from the latter scenario into digging up information for stories, you'll do them a huge favor. Strong research can not only provide facts and figures for a story but also help shape the direction of the story and guide later interviews. In this chapter, the authors give students advice on how to approach story research, where to look for information and on how to think throughout the process.

Discussion Topics

1. Find a single-source story (or more than one) in your school's media outlet or a local news outlet. Remove the byline, then have your students read it at the beginning of class with no explanation and ask them what's wrong with it. Once the class has identified it as a single-source story, discuss the problems inherent with such stories. Then go through the possibilities for additional interviewees and resources to more fully flesh out this story. If possible, find a different outlet's coverage of the same story that included more interviews and other material and compare it to the original story.

2. Students may not realize how valuable librarians can be to reporters doing research. Bring a librarian from your school's library into class, or take the class to the library and meet in a room there. If your library has subject specialists, be sure to find the one for journalism. Go over the resources available to student reporters through the library, both physical and electronic. Ask questions and encourage your students to do the same. Stress to the students that although the Internet is a great resource, there's no one there who will work with you personally on a reporting project (at least not for free).

3. Find one or more examples where news organizations have compiled their own databases and used them to create online interactive features, as noted in the chapter. Go through these with your students stressing the research that was done to make them possible. Emphasize that snappy visuals alone don't make these effective—allowing readers to understand and easily interact with a thicket of data creates and sustains user interest. Actually creating these features is usually beyond the scope of classes using this text, but it's important that students understand the research that goes into putting them together.

4. Go to the Reporters Committee for Freedom of the Press's Open Government Guide (http://www.rcfp.org/open-government-guide). The site lists open records and open meetings laws for all 50 states and the District of Columbia. Go through your state's guidelines with your class, noting areas where your state is either more or less open with public records than others. The site contains a tool that will allow you to compare different elements of public records law among multiple states, so you might compare your state's laws with those of neighboring states.

In-Class Exercises

1. Find the Web site for your city or the largest city near your school. Instruct your students to look up campaign finance records for the city's most recent mayoral election. Have them identify the largest contributors to both the winning and losing candidates, then find basic information about those contributors. If possible, have them find material on other candidates to whom these donors may have contributed.

2. Find out what databases are available to your students through your school (perhaps during a librarian visit to class, as noted previously). Select a person, issue or event important in your area a few years ago. Have your students spend 15 minutes looking up all the information they can find about it on the Internet and make notes. Then have them use the proprietary databases accessible through your school and see how much more information they can find in 15 minutes. Have them write up a synopsis of information they found from each source.

3. Look around online and find two or three unusual news stories that you can verify are true. Then find two or three hoaxes that have been reported as news. Mix these up and put them together in a list for your students. Challenge them to do some research and find out which stories are real and which are fake, and insist that they document their sources for arriving at those conclusions.

4. Have students select a story from local media that relates either to the neighborhood where they live and/or grew up or a subject they know well. Have them use some of the research tools discussed in class or in the chapter to look up additional information on the subject that was absent in the original story and that they believe might have been useful. Have them list these facts and their sources and why they think these extra facts might have made the original story more effective.

Identification Questions

1. Adobe Systems' introduction of the Portable _____ Format, or PDF, allowed for creation of exact copies of documents to be made available online.

2. To write an in-depth story usually requires doing _____ to dig into the factors that led up to an event or its potential consequences.

3. Public _____ are said to track nearly every human activity, from birth to death, from marriage to retirement.

4. More than one reporter has been fooled by an "urban _____," an online hoax that, although entertaining, is ultimately too good to be true.

5. The Freedom of _____ Act protects the right of citizens to examine how their national, state and local governments operate.

6. Providing a detailed look at a topic can involve using computer _____, files containing records and other statistical data.

7. A _____ story—one that doesn't go beyond a single telephone call or press release—can lead to mistakes, unanswered questions, and a loss of public trust.

8. Typing words into a search engine is more formally known as a _____ search.

9. Gathering and using complex statistical data in stories is known as computer-assisted _____.

10. Family keepsakes, letters, photos and yearbooks can all be used as _____ records—personal material that can provide vivid details about someone's life.

ANSWERS: 1: DOCUMENT; 2: RESEARCH; 3: RECORDS; 4: LEGEND; 5: INFORMATION; 6: DATABASES; 7: SINGLE-SOURCE; 8: KEYWORD; 9: REPORTING; 10: PRIVATE.

Web Links

- The Journalist's Toolbox: Public Records (Society of Professional Journalists): http://www.journaliststoolbox.org/archive/public-records/
- In the News Archive (Investigative Reporters and Editors): http://www.ire.org/inthenews_archive/
- Open Government Guide (Reporters Committee for Freedom of the Press): http://www.rcfp.org/open-government-guide
- Uplink Magazine (Investigative Reporters and Editors): http://data.nicar.org/uplink/
- Building a Toolbox for Precision Journalism (*Nieman Reports*): http://www.nieman.harvard.edu/reportsitem.aspx?id=100076

(Note—if a link no longer works, search the title and source of the article to locate it online.)

CHAPTER 8
GRAMMAR, LANGUAGE, STYLE:
USING ACCURATE WORDS

Chapter Summary

A widespread perception exists that in this age of text messages and social networking, grammar and spelling no longer matter. Some of your students may subscribe to this notion, but you need to remind them that writing professionally isn't the same thing as gabbing with your friends. You may find bright, articulate students who understand elements of reporting and storytelling yet whose copy is a minefield. To prepare them for employment and professional success, you'll need to work with them to break bad habits and learn to produce clean copy. In this chapter, the authors discuss elements of grammar and style that students might have long forgotten, along with techniques for producing professional-quality writing on deadline.

Discussion Topics

1. It's not a bad idea to immediately address the issue of whether typos and bad grammar matter in today's society. You may get some students arguing that they don't matter at all anymore—that spelling isn't an indicator of intelligence and that plenty of people they know get by in spite of poor language skills. An effective point of entry for this type of discussion is context. Ask students whether they communicate the same way all the time. Do they write the exact same way they talk? Do they use the same vocabulary in a bar as in church? Perhaps more pointedly, do they know people who don't seem to understand these contextual differences? Another issue that might be raised is development of good habits. If people rarely worry about using the right grammar or spelling, how will they know when they've fouled up something on their résumé, a wedding invitation or some other important document? You might also discuss the "secret handshake" culture of much online communication and how it can lead to misunderstandings and divisions among people.

2. Spend a little time on the Web site for the Bulwer-Lytton Fiction Contest (http://www.bulwer-lytton.com) and select some examples of opaque, overwrought writing from the contest's winners. Put these on the screen or board at the front of your classroom, and invite your students to specifically identify what makes the sentences so gloriously awful. (If you want to turn this into an exercise, have them rewrite the sentences into tight, grammatically correct prose.)

3. Journalistic writing styles are very different from other kinds of writing, especially term papers and other types of assignments. Although it's true that correct spelling and grammar should work across all disciplines, shifting from journalistic style to writing term papers can be difficult. Discuss the differences between these styles in terms of goals and common practices, and raise the question of whether learning to write like a professional journalist helps or hurts in other writing tasks.

4. In your school's news outlet or a local news site, find some examples of material written in the passive voice. Remove any bylines and show them to your students, then discuss how to rewrite each item in the active voice. Then talk about how these changes make sentences tighter and more compelling.

In-Class Exercises

1. Have each of your students call up the Twitter feed of a friend (preferably not a journalism, English or writing major) and look for three to five tweets on the same subject. In this instance, less grammatically correct is better. They can all be written by the friend, or they can be retweets from others. Have them copy the text of each tweet (including hashtags and any other shorthand) and paste it all into their word processor. At the end, have them insert some returns, then have them copy the whole works and paste it following so there are two versions—the original and a version to modify. Have them label the top one "ORIGINAL" and the second one "EDITED." Then have them copyedit the second set of tweets so it makes sense. This should be a fun exercise—if they want to make it multiple sentences, that's fine; and if they want to include rewritten hashtag material in some way, that's also fine. If you want to add another layer, have them paste the original tweets in one more time and run spell-check on them to see what happens.

2. Advertising is notorious for its often lax attitudes about grammar. Do a little Web searching and find some examples of ads that feature ungrammatical slogans, headlines or copy. Present these to your students, have them identify the mistakes, then have them answer these questions: Would using correct grammar ruin the impact of the ad? Does it appear that the poor grammar is being used intentionally to make a point? If so, what is that point?

3. Find a lengthy sample story from a major news outlet and paste its text into your word processor. Insert one copy error into each sentence, rotating among spelling, punctuation and grammar mistakes. Have your students try to find and fix each one, either electronically or on paper. If you have them do it electronically, be sure they don't have access to word processor software with spell-check or grammar-check. Students in the past have been so dependent on these tools that they've risked their semester grades on

exams by trying to secretly look things up on their phones rather than try to get them correct on their own.

4. In addition to journalistic styles and academic styles of writing, students today also deal with a separate lexicon of words and commonalities in the online world. The Yahoo! Style Guide provides a counterpoint to style guides in the other areas of writing by focusing on online terminology and customs. For this exercise, have your students list 10 words specific to online communication and write definitions of what they believe the terms mean. Then have them look up each word in the Yahoo! Style Guide, fill in the guide's definition and briefly discuss the differences between their own understanding of the term and the guide's interpretation.

Identification Questions

1. When you interview professionals and academics about what they do in their jobs, their answers sometimes contain _____, specialized terminology that those within an industry use but that those outside the field might not know.

2. Sentences that lack energy are often written in _____, using weak verbs that simply link the subject of the verb to additional information about the subject rather than expressing action.

3. Effective news writing is _____, like the informal way people talk to their friends every day.

4. In the phrase "That's a huge mistake," the word "huge" is an _____ because it describes the word "mistake."

5. To say "he and his wife is celebrating their wedding anniversary" is incorrect because the subjects of the sentence don't agree with the _____.

6. Connecting two complete sentences to create one single long one is known as a comma _____ and creates a run-on sentence.

7. "As luck would have it" is a _____, one of hundreds of overworked expressions that journalists should avoid in their writing.

8. Effective news writing is _____, focusing on the details that make elements of their stories distinctive and evocative.

9. Whether in a print or digital version, a _____ is vitally important for reporters and editors to use to find answers about spelling, style and word usage.

10. Sentences using _____ are usually engaging and tightly written because they use action verbs and identify the performers of actions.

ANSWERS: 1: JARGON; 2: PASSIVE VOICE; 3: CONVERSATIONAL; 4: ADJECTIVE; 5: VERB; 6: SPLICE; 7: CLICHÉ; 8: SPECIFIC; 9: STYLEBOOK; 10: ACTIVE VOICE.

Web Links

- Cleaning Your Copy: Grammar, Style and More (NewsU):
  http://www.newsu.org/courses/cleaning-your-copy-grammar-style-and-more
- The Yahoo! Style Guide:
  http://styleguide.yahoo.com/
- *Associated Press Stylebook*:
  http://www.apstylebook.com/
- Purdue University Online Writing Lab (OWL):
  http://owl.english.purdue.edu/owl/
- Journalists and Grammar (Stuff Journalists Like blog):
  http://www.stuffjournalistslike.com/2011/11/journalists-and-grammar.html

(Note—if a link no longer works, search the title and source of the article to locate it online.)

CHAPTER 9
NUMBERS: USING ACCURATE FIGURES

Chapter Summary

It's fairly safe to say that few college journalism majors are double majoring in math. Generally students get into journalism because they love to write, yet there comes a point when they need to crunch numbers for an assignment. While this strikes fear in the hearts of many students (and some instructors), a general understanding of a few core concepts will go a long way toward helping them supplement their facts with figures. In this chapter, the authors introduce some basic computations that journalists often use, tie them to practical concepts and show students how to translate statistics into material that readers can understand.

Discussion Topics

1. Find a few examples of news stories that use basic figures (averages, percentages, etc.). Go through the stories with your students and ask what the figures mean. Discuss whether the inclusion of these figures adds value to the story and what the story might lose if they weren't included. If you're teaching a more advanced class, you might find stories that include some more complex calculations and talk about how they make certain concepts more understandable or more concrete than if they were left out.

2. Look in local or regional news outlets in your area to find a story that uses numbers effectively, whether simple percentages or more complex calculations. Then, from a different outlet or reporter, find another version of the same story that doesn't use figures much or at all. Have your class read both versions and discuss whether they believe the story that included statistics was more effective. Did the numbers add to the students' understanding of the story subject? Did they not make much of an impact? Or did they serve more to confuse than clarify?

3. Federal, state and university budgets are seemingly always in the news, but most college students are primarily worried about survival between paychecks. Go over some of the fundamentals of budgets with them—deficits, debt and surplus; revenues and expenditures; funding sources and stipulations; and why lawmakers can seemingly never get a budget deal done on time. If you teach at a public institution, show the students some of the basic elements of your school's budget and talk about how money is allotted and spent across campus.

4. In this age of information overload, it's not uncommon to read the occasional news story containing enough statistics to make your head spin. The question for every journalist should be, "How much is too much?" Find some examples that you believe take number crunching a bit too far for the average reader and use them to start a class discussion on appropriate and inappropriate use of numbers in news stories. Be sure to talk about the subject matter, intended audience and nature of the publication as well as what types of figures are useful for specific purposes.

In-Class Exercises

1. Lead your students in a little calculation exercise. First, count aloud how many students are in class. Second, ask a few questions aloud and have students calculate and write down their answers (stress that there should be no help from computers or smartphones). You can allow them to use their textbooks as guides to help them calculate these figures if you like. Have all the left-handed students raise their hands and have each student calculate what percentage of the class is left-handed. Have all the students with brown eyes raise their hands, then blue, then green, then "other" (if needed), and have students calculate those percentages. If the class is small enough, have each student name off his/her number of siblings, then have the students calculate the average (mean) number of siblings per student. Have each student say his/her age aloud, then ask the students to compute the mode of these figures—they'll need to have jotted down each value one by one for this, and it's up to you whether you want to remind them of this beforehand. The purpose here isn't to teach high-level math skills but to demystify these processes and make students comfortable with basic calculations.

2. Have your students call up a local news outlet's Web site. Give them 30 minutes to look through the top 10 stories on the site (using whatever definition you prefer) to analyze their use of numbers. For each of the 10 stories, have each student write up (a) whether the story used numbers; (b) if so, in what ways and how extensively they were used; and (c) if not, whether there was a way that numbers could have been used to enhance the story.

3. Break the class up into groups of three or more. Give the groups 15–20 minutes to assemble as much statistical information as they can about themselves in whatever categories they like. Encourage them to be creative beyond the standard age, gender, ethnicity and the like. What percentage of them have tattoos? How many have been to Europe or Asia? What's their median age? Do a majority of them have webbed toes? Beyond this, encourage a little statistical creativity if they're up to it. For example, if there happen to be three left-handers in a group of four people, what's the statistical probability of that? When they're finished, go around the room and have each group

present a "statistical profile" of their group, including both basic demographics and the more unusual stats they've compiled.

Identification Questions

1. In a list of numbers, the _____ is the number that appears most often.

2. Numbers that relate to life, health, disease and death are usually referred to as _____ statistics.

3. Whereas journalists are almost always skilled at expressing themselves verbally and in writing, many news staffs are full of _____, people who don't deal comfortably with numbers or calculations.

4. In polls and surveys, _____ error refers to the statistical likelihood of accuracy based on probability sampling of a population.

5. A story that uses statistical analysis to suggest correlation or causation between two social phenomena generally uses _____ statistics, such as a t-test or ANOVA.

6. The _____ income in an area is the rate of yearly wages per person in that area.

7. A portion of an entire quantity or group expressed in one-hundredths is a _____.

8. When you compare the current monetary value of an item to what it was worth a certain number of years ago, you need to adjust for _____, an increase in the price of goods and services.

9. Instead of an average, the _____ of a group of numbers is the middle figure in terms of size, which is useful when the list contains one or more extreme cases.

10. _____ measurements sort things into categories (men and women, Democrats and Republicans, etc.) to help simplify and deepen understanding of a set of numbers.

ANSWERS: 1: MODE; 2: VITAL; 3: INNUMERATES; 4: SAMPLING; 5: INFERENTIAL; 6: PER CAPITA; 7: PERCENTAGE; 8: INFLATION; 9: MEDIAN; 10: NOMINAL.

Web Links

- U.S. Bureau of Labor Statistics' Inflation and Prices calculator: http://www.bls.gov/bls/inflation.htm
- Math for Journalists: Help With Numbers (NewsU): http://www.newsu.org/courses/math-journalists
- Understanding statistics: A journalist's guide (Knight Center): http://knightcenter.utexas.edu/blog/understanding-statistics-journalists-guide
- The Curious Science of Counting a Crowd (*Popular Mechanics*): http://www.popularmechanics.com/science/the-curious-science-of-counting-a-crowd
- Math for journalists (Journalist's Resource): http://journalistsresource.org/reference/foundations/math-for-journalists/

(Note—if a link no longer works, search the title and source of the article to locate it online.)

CHAPTER 10
LEAD WRITING

Chapter Summary

Most college-level journalism instructors have been reporters, and if there's one thing reporters pride themselves on, it's writing leads. A combination of skill and repetition means most professional reporters can write a lead under nearly any circumstances. This can invite frustration as a teacher when students don't instinctively know how to find the central element of a story that will grab the reader's attention. In this chapter, the authors aim to familiarize students with the process of writing leads, how to use different styles of leads to suit different purposes, and how the nut graf can be a useful tool in enhancing the beginning of a story.

Discussion Topics

1. Reporters are forever talking to each other about stories they've covered. A common practice is telling a friend a scenario and asking "What's your lead?" Find five stories with interesting scenarios in local media outlets, distill each down to its central facts, and present them to your class. In each case, read off the facts and ask the group, "What's your lead?" Take student suggestions for these, discuss types of leads that might work and different approaches to the story that might attract readers.

2. If your classroom has a screen in the front, show a local news outlet's Web site on it. Based on nothing more than the headline, ask students about possible types of leads for various stories, then look at them and see what approach the writer has taken. Based on the additional material from the story, ask the students what other types of leads might work in each case, and talk about how they might be phrased to best engage readers.

3. As noted in the chapter, journalism is often criticized for focusing on conflict (wars, crime, political differences, violence etc.). Yet the best leads seldom contain actual conflict but rather tension between multiple parties, which introduces drama and entices the user to read further. Students often confuse the terms "tension" and "conflict," so talk to your students about the differences between the two and why they matter so much in storytelling.

4. Leads have traditionally been vitally important in news writing because readers could be counted on to read the first paragraph of a story if nothing else. In today's media marketplace, however, readers often get no farther than the headline or a brief blurb about

a story. In spite of this, story leads are still seen as vitally important throughout journalism. Discuss this with your students, and ask them to relate the question to their own news-reading habits.

In-Class Exercises

1. Have your students go to the Web site of a local media outlet and select three news stories. Have them deconstruct the lead to each story as outlined in the chapter, breaking down the five W's, the H and the SW for each. Then have them write a sentence or two on how effective they believe the lead is, how they might change it if they were writing the story and why.

2. Make a list of magazine Web sites or other sites that run lengthy feature stories. Let each student choose a site from that list, then have them pick three stories from that site. Instruct them to identify the type of lead used in each story, then rewrite the lead using a different style. Allow them to use material from elsewhere in the story if they think it would improve the lead. Have them also briefly explain why they chose the style they did for each rewrite.

3. Find three to five different versions of the same news story in local, regional or national media outlets. For this assignment, the more they differ from each other, the better, especially if they use different styles of leads. Have your students read these and, based on the information they find in all the stories, write their own lead. Also have them explain why they chose the style and facts they did. If you like, you could have them write their own leads in two different styles and rank the two as their first and second choices.

Identification Questions

1. One way to attract readers with a lead is to introduce _____, a condition that exists when two or more forces operate at cross purposes.

2. Reporters should avoid _____ leads, which use overworked familiar phrases, because they can drain the energy from what might otherwise be a compelling story.

3. Journalists shouldn't be afraid to _____ their leads after writing them because sometimes the best leads require detailed work.

4. A lead that uses a single instance or individual to illustrate a larger issue is called an _____ lead.

5. In the "Five W's, an H and a SW" method of writing leads, H stands for _____.

6. A _____ lead provides a synopsis of the main facts of the story.

7. The news media are criticized, often justifiably, for their preoccupation with _____ when opponents attack each other.

8. A lead that introduces characters into a scene, begins telling their story and shows them facing some kind of complication is known as a _____ lead.

9. Choosing the right lead for a story often depends on three conditions: _____, audience needs and exclusivity.

10. One way to see how the elements of a lead are used in a story is to _____ the lead, to take it apart and see where the central questions are answered.

ANSWERS: 1: TENSION; 2: CLICHÉD; 3: REVISE; 4: EMBLEM; 5: HOW; 6: SUMMARY; 7: CONFLICT; 8: NARRATIVE; 9: TIME; 10: DECONSTRUCT.

Web Links

- The Lead Lab (NewsU):
  http://www.newsu.org/courses/lead-lab
- The 5 W's (and How) of writing for the Web (Steve Buttry):
  http://stevebuttry.wordpress.com/2011/11/14/the-5-ws-and-how-of-writing-for-the-web/
- Selling the Power of Focus (Chip Scanlan, Poynter):
  http://www.poynter.org/how-tos/newsgathering-storytelling/chip-on-your-shoulder/18481/selling-the-power-of-focus/
- Feature Leads (Richard Craig):
  http://www.jmc.sjsu.edu/faculty/rcraig/featureleads.html

(Note—if a link no longer works, search the title and source of the article to locate it online.)

CHAPTER 11
STORY FORMS

Chapter Summary

Whereas different forms of leads are often easy for students to comprehend, different story structures are sometimes harder for them to grasp. Leads are the quick hook, but structures are the true body of a story, and writers need to make sure their structures serve the facts of the story and the realities of the interviews and other materials that are available. If there's one storytelling element that students sometimes resist, it's set story structures because they're perceived to inhibit creativity. In this chapter, the authors familiarize them with many kinds of story forms; but as the instructor it will be your job to show how knowing these structures can enhance their ability to tell stories, especially on deadline.

Discussion Topics

1. Given that students are sometimes reticent to learn traditional story structures because they're perceived to limit creativity, this is something you should address right away. Stress to them that a story form is simply a mold into which you pour the content of stories and that readers won't notice the structure. Rather, a well-structured story compels them to continue reading. Discuss this and show some examples of stories with different structures to illustrate these points and others you may wish to make.

2. Reporters often complain about the inverted pyramid, yet it remains the most common story form in daily American professional journalism. Because of this, it's a form in which young journalists must show proficiency if they are to get jobs. Discuss the inverted pyramid's strengths and weaknesses with your class, and elaborate on why mastery of the form still matters in the digital age.

3. A certain percentage of students who major in journalism seem to be misplaced novelists. While the daily grind of reporting might not be their ideal scenario, they are often drawn to long-form feature stories and to more narrative story forms. Discuss how certain forms lend themselves more to this type of storytelling, but also talk about why it's not appropriate for every news story.

4. On your own, find some online news sites that offer truly different story forms—not necessarily tweet-sized chunks but different methods of storytelling. Select some you find interesting and share them with your class. Discuss the types of stories that are served

well by these forms, and ask your students if they find such forms appealing. Have them be as specific as possible about what they like or don't like, especially if there's division among the students over preferred forms.

In-Class Exercises

1. Locate some examples of stories with the forms discussed in the chapter. Present the stories to your students, identify their forms and have the students go through them to identify the story segments that make up the form's component parts. For example, in an hourglass story, have students identify the top, turn and narrative.

2. Find a lengthy news story with lots of elements and distill it down into its bare facts and quotes. Give that material to your students, and have them use the Five Boxes technique to organize the material and write it up into a new story in 20–30 minutes.

3. The serial narrative form is frequently used for in-depth stories that require lots of space, to enable news outlets to spread them out over several days. Traditionally this has been because of a lack of space in newspapers, but the online medium has no such concerns. Find a long-form feature story in an online outlet and have your students rewrite it as a serial narrative, explaining at the end why they made the changes they did.

Identification Questions

1. The " _____ " can refer to a paragraph within a story that provides details and context for the narrative or to a story form that features it prominently.

2. Many online news outlets encourage their writers to write in _____—small blocks of information that are quickly and easily read by users who move quickly through different news Web sites.

3. In the _____ form, a lengthy story is broken up into segments and is revealed gradually, usually over days or weeks.

4. One way to quickly organize a story is to use five _____ containing different story elements, creating a simple outline that gives writers an idea of where to put information.

5. A piece of technology from the mid-1800s that changed news story forms was the _____, which encouraged writers to get to the point quickly.

6. In the narrative story form, in the beginning the writer sets a _____, much as would happen in a movie or play.

7. The _____ form has three parts—a top, a turn and a narrative—and is flexible enough to be useful covering many different types of stories.

8. Writing a news story that includes bullet points and subheads is one of a number of different _____ story forms.

9. The most common traditional news story form, the _____, puts the most newsworthy information at the top, with the remaining information following in order of importance.

10. A popular digital technology, _____, is used by many reporters to update breaking news stories but isn't generally considered a story form because of its truncated nature.

ANSWERS: 1: NUT GRAF; 2: CHUNKS; 3: SERIAL NARRATIVE; 4: BOXES; 5: TELEGRAPH; 6: SCENE; 7: HOURGLASS; 8: ALTERNATIVE; 9: INVERTED PYRAMID; 10: TWITTER.

Web Links

- The Inverted Pyramid (Stuff Journalists Like blog):
  http://www.stuffjournalistslike.com/2009/04/inverted-pyramids.html
- Inverted Pyramid Checklist (JProf):
  http://www.jprof.com/writing/invertedpyramidchecklist.html
- Beyond the Inverted Pyramid: Creating Alternative Story Forms (NewsU):
  http://www.newsu.org/courses/beyond-inverted-pyramid-creating-alternative-story
- Forms/Narratives (J-Storytelling.com—Steven Strasser):
  http://j-storytelling.com/category/forms/

(Note—if a link no longer works, search the title and source of the article to locate it online.)

CHAPTER 12
WRITING FOR PRINT

Chapter Summary

In the digital age, it might be difficult to convince some students that they'll probably write for a print newspaper or magazine at some point. In spite of the so-called death of print, local newspapers in many areas continue to thrive and continue to provide many journalism students with their first jobs or first internships. College newspapers continue to sell more advertising for their print editions than online, and in many ways a daily print paper is the best training ground prospective reporters can get. In learning the essentials of writing for print outlets, you gain skills transferrable to any writing task. Thus, it's not a bad idea to prepare your students to write for a print publication, even if some of them never read anything that isn't on their phones.

Discussion Topics

1. Bring in some local and/or national print newspapers. Ask them how the print and online editions might differ—students may assume that a print newspaper is identical to its online counterpart. Then go through the print editions, preferably with their Web sites on a screen behind you. Discuss the differences in how they're organized, what content is featured, how stories are edited, how headlines differ and other elements.

2. One major difference between writing for newspapers and Web sites is the deadline structure. For decades, newspaper writers had one deadline for all their stories to be done every day (aside from days when a major story might provoke editors to produce an extra edition). Ask your students how they think this might have changed news reporting for good or bad, and discuss whether the constant news deadline for online news is better or worse for consumers.

3. Newspaper layout and graphics have evolved a great deal over time, especially since 1980 or so. The increased use of color and the use of computers to give page designers more control have made newspapers far more visually stimulating than ever before. Discuss this with your students and perhaps show some examples of the evolution of newspaper design. Having said this, given that this is presumably a writing class, raise the question of whether these improvements in graphics have served to steer more readers toward stories on the page or distract them away from stories.

4. Editorials are a newspaper tradition dating to the beginnings of the medium. Yet students might well confuse them with op-ed columns or regular news coverage. Given the prevalence of opinion-based blogging and commentary online, they might not know the specific characteristics of editorials. Discuss how editorials are written, what they represent and their place within the opinion section and the newspaper as a whole.

In-Class Exercises

1. Some newspaper readers have gravitated to online news in recent years, but others still choose to get their news on paper. Whether it's simple familiarity, the tactile nature of a newspaper, the opening of sections, the scanning of headlines or other elements, some readers simply prefer the experience of reading a newspaper. With that in mind, tell students in advance to bring in a print copy of a newspaper to your next class. Once they've arrived, tell them to spend 20–30 minutes reading the paper, then have them write about the actual experience of reading a print paper and how it differs from other ways of getting news. Stress that they should be specific about all aspects of reading the paper, not just the content.

2. Find an example of a major story that's covered by a newspaper with both a straight news report and a news analysis. Have your students read both and write a couple of paragraphs on the similarities and differences between the two. How much documented factual content and how much opinion are found in the analysis piece? Is there any of the author's opinion in the news story? Should the analysis be on the opinion page or at least labeled as opinion in the paper?

3. One reason local newspapers have continued to thrive is by acting as the main sources of information about their communities. In some cases, this means finding local angles for national stories. Find three national stories with possibilities for local angles, present them to your students and have the students write up how they would localize the stories, who they might interview and how their first couple of paragraphs might read.

Identification Questions

1. A newspaper's _____ is the average number of copies distributed in a day

2. Young journalists often get their first professional experience as _____, working in news roles for a limited period of time.

3. News _____ are stories in which reporters or editors who are experts on a subject interpret complex trends or developments for readers, sometimes including their opinions.

4. The portion of a newspaper devoted to news content—not advertising—is referred to as the _____, which needs to be filled with news and information every day.

5. A newspaper's chief management figure is the _____ who oversees the newsroom, editorial pages and business departments.

6. Newspaper companies are generally divided into two parts, referred to as the editorial and _____ sides.

7. A good way for local newspapers to get a story out of national news is to _____ a national trend, to give it an angle your readers will recognize.

8. Among the fastest growing segments of the newspaper business are _____ publications, which provide news to immigrant communities that may or may not speak English.

9. A newspaper's top editor, generally known as the _____, oversees publication of the paper and represents the editorial departments as a member of the senior management team.

10. Newspaper advertising and circulation sales forces sell _____, including both small and full-page display advertisements.

ANSWERS: 1: CIRCULATION; 2: INTERNS; 3: ANALYSES; 4: NEWS HOLE; 5: PUBLISHER; 6: BUSINESS; 7: LOCALIZE; 8: ETHNIC; 9: EDITOR-IN-CHIEF; 10: AD SPACE.

Web Links

- Glossary of Newspaper Terms (*Brownsville Herald* NIE): http://nie.brownsvilleherald.com/newspaperterms.htm
- American Society of Newspaper Editors: http://asne.org/
- The Daily Miracle (Newspapers in Education): http://www.nieworld.com/cc/NewspaperADailyMiracle.pdf

(Note—if a link no longer works, search the title and source of the article to locate it online.)

CHAPTER 13
ONLINE WRITING AND
CONTENT PRODUCTION

Chapter Summary

Do your students' lives seem to revolve around their computers and electronic devices? This certainly seems to be the case for a huge percentage of young people in today's digital age. With that in mind, it might be surprising that some journalism students seem ambivalent about learning the skills needed to succeed in online journalism. Some don't want to be bothered with learning video or photo skills—they just want to write. In this chapter, the authors' goal isn't really to teach them specific pieces of software, as those seem to change every year. The idea is to learn a way of thinking that they can apply to their reporting and editing, regardless of the programs they use to create content.

Discussion Topics

1. Today's young people have been raised in a multimedia environment and seem to take it for granted, yet when it comes to creating multimedia content some of them seem surprisingly fearful. Although your class might not actually create multimedia content, it's useful to address this trepidation quickly in the online portion of the class. Ask your students about how they tell stories, what multimedia technologies they've used to tell them and what aspects other technologies might add to them.

2. Story comments are a staple of the online news world, a facet that allows readers to participate in a conversation rather than simply reading an article. Too often, especially in recent years, they get hijacked by people complaining about the author or the subject, or seemingly just stirring up arguments for the fun of it. Your students have undoubtedly read these over the years and perhaps even contributed comments of their own. Discuss what commenting adds to online news stories and whether they believe commenting is a good or bad thing overall. You might also mention that because of assorted abuses of commenting, many news organizations are now either requiring commenters to register with their sites, moderating comments before they're posted, or doing away with commenting altogether.

3. When multimedia storytelling is done well, its different elements complement each other and blend together to create a unified news package. Yet each piece of the package was the result of a choice made by the people who created it. Talk with your students about

the storytelling strengths of different multimedia elements used in online news. What types of material are best presented in what formats? What characteristics do these technologies have that make them effective for certain storytelling functions?

4. Bloggers have become sources of controversy in the news business. In previous generations journalists might develop followings after being hired by news organizations and establishing their reputations over many years, but today anyone can create a blog and start publishing without developing journalistic credentials first. Ask your students whether this is good or bad—does this democratize journalism or cheapen it?

In-Class Exercises

1. Provide your students with examples of three to five news stories, either in print or PDF format, which lend themselves to linking to related Web sites but contain no links. Have each student make up a list of five or more links, including the URLs, to Web sites that might provide useful background or supplemental information about each story. For each link, have them say briefly what this Web site might add to the story.

2. Students today get their news from a variety of sources, some of which are traditional news organizations (local and national outlets, with staffs of editors and reporters) and some of which are anything but traditional. Have your students list a minimum of five Web sites where they get their news, and have them be specific about what they get from each site and why they believe it has credibility. Stress that they should be completely honest and not restrict themselves to listing traditional sites—the definition of news applied here should be theirs alone.

3. Find some examples of online news stories that feature both content created by professional journalists and submitted by users. Present these to your students and have them write up their opinions of the strengths and weaknesses of both kinds of content. Is the professional content more compelling because it's been more thoroughly and exhaustively prepared, or is the amateur content more interesting precisely because it's less polished and therefore more "real"?

4. Web sites for many local TV stations have become venues for "converged" journalism, as they contain both text and video stories and sometimes still photo galleries and other content. Go online and find some good examples from local TV stations of news stories containing multiple kinds of content. Show these to your students and have them write up how well they believe the different elements of the story complement each other. Is the text story stronger or weaker than a comparable newspaper story? Is the video

exceptionally compelling? Are there any elements that don't add much to the story? What might they do differently in presenting the story?

Identification Questions

1. A common technology on news Web sites is the _____, which merges photos, text and sound.

2. A brief news summary generally called a _____ is a sentence beneath a headline quickly describing a news story.

3. As news moved from traditional print and broadcast to the online platform, the concept of _____—print and broadcast journalists working together to produce multimedia content—became popular.

4. An important function on the business side of online news outlets is known by the initials _____, making the site compatible for major search engines so that the stories and news content show higher up in keyword searches.

5. In spite of the ever-evolving electronic technologies for creating and presenting news content, online reporters still need to learn the _____ of journalism—how to gather and verify news and information and deliver it with clarity and precision.

6. Whereas print reporters traditionally outlined stories before putting them together, online journalists today sometimes create _____, which define not only the facts and figures but also the media elements and resources to be used.

7. Journalists who use computers and other electronic devices to file their reports directly from the field have been nicknamed "_____."

8. Because of the different skills involved, _____ with other journalists to create reporting teams has become common in online journalism.

9. A common practice on some newspaper Web sites has been _____ content, simply copying it from the print edition to the online edition.

10. The multimedia element that truly makes online stories unique—the clickable _____—allows journalists to supplement their stories with material from elsewhere on the Internet.

ANSWERS: 1: AUDIO SLIDESHOW; 2: BLURB; 3: CONVERGENCE; 4: SEO; 5: FUNDAMENTALS; 6: STORYBOARDS; 7: MOJOS; 8: COLLABORATION; 9: REPURPOSING; 10: LINK/HYPERLINK.

Web Links

- Journalists' Toolbox (Society of Professional Journalists): http://www.journaliststoolbox.org/
- OJR: The Online Journalism Review: http://www.ojr.org/
- Online News Association: http://journalists.org/
- *New York Times* interactive features: http://query.nytimes.com/search/sitesearch/#/interactive+feature
- Interactive Graphics (E-Learning Examples blog): http://elearningexamples.com/examples/interactive-graphics/
- Removing Content: When to Unring the Bell? (Poynter.org): http://www.poynter.org/column.asp?id=101&aid=129083

(Note—if a link no longer works, search the title and source of the article to locate it online.)

CHAPTER 14
BROADCAST WRITING

Chapter Summary

With newspapers increasingly entering agreements with TV stations to share content, the convergence of news we've long anticipated is finally becoming reality. As such, young reporters may find themselves writing for video rather than just for text stories. Broadcast journalism has its own language and procedures that your students might not know. In this chapter, the authors introduce the basic elements of broadcast storytelling and discuss some of the strengths, weaknesses and challenges inherent to the medium.

Discussion Topics

1. A general rule for good interviewing for text stories is to use open-ended questions—ones without a prescribed answer—to get your interviewees to speak freely in their answers. In broadcast news, however, open-ended questions are seen as a bad thing. Introduce this apparent contradiction to your students, and ask them why this divide might exist. Discuss the differences between the characteristics of broadcast and print stories and how those differences might contribute to this divide and also shape the nature of interviews in each discipline.

2. Visuals matter greatly in news—research shows that photos, design and video attract audience attention. In particular, TV news has the reputation of putting visuals above all else, yet even in the digital age it's still the most popular news source in America. Raise this issue with your students and see if they hold this "style over substance" view of television news or whether its video content and live coverage of breaking news give it credibility as more "real" than other formats.

3. The term "producer" has long been commonly used in broadcast news, generally because of the technical aspects of putting together media elements for newscasts. In recent years, the term "producer" has become a job title in online news—it's common to see openings for Web producers, content producers and the like throughout the industry. Talk to your students about what the term "producer" implies about a job and whether the title is appropriate in online or even print newsrooms.

4. Edward R. Murrow famously said that television "can teach, it can illuminate; yes, and it can even inspire. But it can do so only to the extent that humans are determined to use it

to those ends. Otherwise it is merely wires and lights in a box." At the time he said this, TV news was barely a decade old. Now, more than 50 years later, TV news has evolved tremendously, yet Murrow's concerns still resonate. Ask your students whether they think Murrow's quote is still relevant to TV news, and discuss whether the issues he raised are more or less appropriate than they were when he delivered them in 1958.

In-Class Exercises

1. It's generally understood that the text of broadcast stories is far shorter than the average newspaper story. The book discusses some of the reasons why, and you should talk about these reasons in class. For this exercise, find three news stories covered by both TV and print/online outlets in your area. Get transcripts of the TV stories, either by transcribing them yourself, finding them on a database service such as Lexis-Nexis or copying them from the TV station's Web site if available. Give these sets of TV transcripts and print stories to your students and have them discuss the differences in how they're written. Have them discuss the differences in length and how TV's use of video and audio helps fill in gaps that may exist in the text.

2. The chapter lists a lot of terminology used in broadcast news. Record (or find online) a half-hour TV newscast and have your students deconstruct its stories to find examples of these terms. You can simply have the students take the terms from the book or you can make a list on your own. Have them note the points in various stories when they see examples of these terms, and note the purpose of each type of content in the context in which it is used.

3. Online news has been described as a hybrid of all the news formats that came before it. In particular, because of the use of video, it's been frequently compared to TV news, but the two platforms have as many differences as similarities. Have your students discuss the similarities and differences between TV and online news in terms of reporting, deadlines, presentation and any other relevant categories. In addition, have them write about the two forms in terms of credibility—is one inherently more or less believable than the other?

Identification Questions

1. Broadcast news scripts are generally written in a _____ format, in two columns.

2. Radio journalists use a digital audio recorder and microphone to record _____, comments that print reporters call quotes.

3. TV reporters frequently conduct _____ to identify the best sources for a story before talking to them on camera.

4. The end of a television news story is referred to as a _____.

5. In TV news, a complete story is called a _____ because it's told with audio and video clips, plus graphics, animation and video effects.

6. Television news scripts are written in _____ to be easier to read, except for words spoken by persons in prerecorded interview clips.

7. Interviews and other audio and video content in broadcast news must be _____, or transcribed verbatim.

8. In TV news stories, _____ refers to the words spoken by the reporter, anchor or sources whose comments have been prerecorded.

9. Unlike reporters in other media, TV reporters must worry about their _____ on camera, to avoid detracting from the credibility of their stories.

10. The introduction to a broadcast news story, often read by an anchor, is known as the _____.

ANSWERS: 1: SPLIT PAGE; 2: ACTUALITIES; 3: PRE-INTERVIEWS; 4: TAG/CLOSE; 5: PACKAGE; 6: ALL CAPS; 7: LOGGED; 8: NARRATION; 9: APPEARANCE; 10: LEAD-IN.

Web Links

- How to Write for News Radio (Suite 101 blog):
  http://suite101.com/article/writing-for-news-radio-a62727
- The 10 rules of writing news for television (Jessica Grillanda, Canadian Journalism Project):
  http://j-source.ca/article/10-rules-writing-news-television
- Top Tips of the Trade (Mervin Block Television Newswriting Workshop):
  http://www.mervinblock.com/?q=node/29
- Questions to Consider Before Airing 911 calls (Al Tompkins, Poynter):
  http://www.poynter.org/uncategorized/11557/questions-to-consider-before-airing-911-calls/

(Note—if a link no longer works, search the title and source of the article to locate it online.)

CHAPTER 15
DIVERSITY

Chapter Summary

The concept of diversity in terms of race, ethnicity, sexuality and other issues is widely considered a minefield by many journalists—they see it as something that's complicated or will get them in trouble. In a way, though, students may be ahead of professionals on this issue. As American society has become more multicultural, younger generations have generally become more tolerant of people different from themselves. Having said this, a lack of understanding of relevant issues can cause anguish both inside and outside the newsroom. Worse still, a lack of inclusion can result in news coverage that neglects issues important to significant segments of the audience.

Discussion Topics

1. One good way to start out a discussion on diversity is to ask students whether they've ever felt they were being treated in a particular way because of a personal characteristic. Sometimes this produces fairly obvious responses and sometimes not. If the discussion isn't as active as you'd prefer, you can take the subject to great lengths. Some students with names that are difficult to spell or pronounce feel that this hurts them socially. The same can happen with students that are especially tall or short. If students have been the only one in their class to have a particular trait, have them talk about it. Having said all this, a useful question to those who respond is this: Do they feel at times as if their unusual attribute or characteristic has come to dominate their identity? Do they want to be treated as a whole person, not just someone with this trait? From there, tell them to imagine they're being interviewed—would they want a reporter to dismiss their opinions because of one trait?

2. When a news event happens in a community that doesn't often receive much media attention, journalists are sometimes criticized for "parachuting in" to the area, getting a few interviews and photos, then writing stories that make it sound like they're in touch with the community. Ask your students whether this has happened in their neighborhoods at some point, and discuss ways that reporters can improve this perception and report more accurately from these communities.

3. Some of the most interesting items brought up in discussions of diversity come from students' own lives. Ask the group to share examples where, as children or young adults,

they've been confronted with an issue that involved trying to overcome, understand or deal with differences in race, gender, sexual preference, disability or similar issues. To soften the ground for such potentially sensitive topics, it's a good idea to share a story of your own with the class, and to stress that the discussion begin with an assumption of mutual respect. Be ready to place examples into the context of journalism where appropriate—how would you represent the issues behind some of these anecdotes in news stories?

4. Ask the students for an honest assessment of your college/university. Is it truly a diverse place in terms of the issues discussed in the chapter? Would it be characterized as an inclusive or exclusive place overall? Do classes of students mix with others or keep to themselves? Are there areas that could be improved? Perhaps most important, are your school's student media reflecting these campus realities? This is the type of discussion that could dominate an entire class period, but it should also be productive—use it as a springboard to come up with class activities and projects specific to your school.

In-Class Exercises

1. In local or regional news outlets, find one or more examples where different outlets covered the same event within a minority community. Ideally, one outlet would cover the event very differently from the other. Have your students compare one outlet's coverage to the other's and discuss how well each story dealt with some of the issues discussed in the chapter. Did one outlet seem to have been more thorough in including context and multiple points of view? Did both outlets seem to make a good-faith effort at getting across cultural specifics to help readers understand the context of the event?

2. Break up the class into groups of two or three. Have the students talk to the other members of their group about elements of the culture in which they were brought up that might be considered unusual. These can relate to anything from ethnic culture to simple family quirks—whatever the students choose is generally fine. Have them write up brief synopses of their classmates' examples and how they might work those elements into a story about the student's family. This can be as serious or as light as you prefer—even silly examples are useful in reminding young journalists to seek context before they write.

3. Challenge your students to come up with an idea for an "untold story" from their own neighborhood. Have them try to come up with an idea that's specific to the culture of where they grew up and that might not otherwise be told. Instruct them to come up with perhaps three general concepts, select the one they like the best and then write up a proposal for a story.

Identification Questions

1. Reflexive ways of reporting that rely on stereotyped perceptions are referred to as clichés of _____.

2. Reporters can get a better understanding of minority communities through _____—by spending lots of time getting to know the communities, the people and the issues important to them.

3. News stories that cover the accomplishments of an ethnic community or individual as if astonished that someone like this could be successful are called "_____" stories.

4. One way reporters can avoid problems is to have their stories checked for a lack of _____ by a colleague belonging to the group covered in the story.

5. Learning about the culture, values and norms of a community is called cultural _____, which makes it possible for journalists to look beyond themselves to recognize and appreciate those different from them.

6. Reporter and editor Aly Colón has encouraged journalists to broaden their cultural horizons by answering five Ws of _____ to help others tell untold stories in their communities.

7. Some reporters find it useful to keep a "_____" that enables them to find diverse sources that reflect a range of experiences and viewpoints.

8. Terms used in news stories to classify someone by race are known as racial _____.

9. A common problem in attempts at diverse reporting is _____, the act of letting a single person within a minority group speak for the whole group.

10. A good way to avoid letting euphemisms, stereotypes and clichés sneak into your reporting is to use _____, using specific language rather than broad, catch-all terms.

ANSWERS: 1: VISION; 2: IMMERSION; 3: GEE WHIZ; 4: SENSITIVITY; 5: COMPETENCE; 6: DIVERSITY; 7: RAINBOW ROLODEX; 8: IDENTIFIERS; 9: TOKENISM; 10: PRECISION.

Web Links

- Diversity resources (Society of Professional Journalists): http://www.spj.org/diversity.asp
- Organizations Supporting Diversity in Journalism (Maynard Institute): http://www.maynardije.org/organizations
- National Lesbian & Gay Journalists Association stylebook supplement on lesbian, gay, bisexual & transgender terminology: http://www.nlgja.org/files/NLGJAStylebook0712.pdf
- Diversity at Work (Poynter): http://www.poynter.org/category/how-tos/newsgathering-storytelling/diversity-at-work/

(Note—if a link no longer works, search the title and source of the article to locate it online.)

CHAPTER 16
LIBEL, PRIVACY, ETHICS

Chapter Summary

Unless students have already taken a media law class, this chapter is frequently an eye-opener. Even students who have worked in campus media seldom have the faintest notion of what happens when lawyers get involved with journalism. Being fearless about printing truth is a lot easier once you understand libel laws and legal protections. In this chapter, the authors discuss both legal issues and ethical behavior that can keep journalists from moral and ethical lapses.

Discussion Topics

1. Go over the differences between libel and slander with your class. The evolution of these terms in American history is especially interesting given the nature of some of the court cases involved. Of particular note are laws from the last 50 years or so, which created different standards for public figures. Discuss the concept of fair comment and criticism, and then ask the class whether public figures should have to meet a higher standard. At this point, another question begs to be asked: In the age of reality TV, YouTube and Facebook, exactly what constitutes a public figure?

2. Nearly every reporter has been through a situation where someone agrees to an interview, then sees the result published, gets angry and either denies saying something, complains that it was taken out of context or says "I didn't mean it like that." Worse still is when they comment on the story online and make you look bad. Few of these ever result in legal action, but they can cause stress and take time away from your job. Discuss ways that reporters can avoid such scenarios, whether transcribing interviews immediately, recording interviews or contacting interviewees and reading quotes back to them.

3. Examples of fabrication in journalism are sadly plentiful. The famous examples of Jayson Blair, Stephen Glass and Janet Cooke are just a few instances where reporters fabricated details, quotes or whole stories for the sake of creating drama. Choose two or three examples of these and show them to the class. Many are compelling and well written, showing that these are talented writers. Ask the group whether these stories sound like they could be true or whether something about them rings false.

4. Ethical cases are great for getting students to think about the repercussions of what journalists do and usually make for interesting classroom exchanges. There are plenty of

examples of these available online for you to choose from, most notably at the Web sites of Indiana University (http://journalism.indiana.edu/resources/ethics), the Poynter Institute (http://www.poynter.org/how-tos/10532/tip-sheets-ethics-1994-2010/) and the Society of Professional Journalists (http://www.spj.org/ethicscasestudies.asp). Ask your students to say what they would do in these scenarios, and encourage disagreement and debate. Most students enjoy these exchanges greatly and gain a great deal from them.

In-Class Exercises

1. The case of Crystal Cox, an Oregon blogger, has drawn much attention among journalists and Internet users. Cox was sued for defamation by the Obsidian Finance Group, an investment firm, for writing blog posts that criticized the firm and its founder. A U.S. District Court judge ruled that Cox was not protected by shield laws governing journalism because she was not "affiliated with any newspaper, magazine, periodical, book, pamphlet, news service, wire service, news or feature syndicate, broadcast station or network, or cable television system." In effect, the court ruled that bloggers aren't journalists and are therefore exempt from laws protecting reporters. Invite students to look up information on this case, then discuss whether they think the court's ruling is justified and why or why not.

2. Journalists pride themselves on accuracy, yet libel law allows for a certain amount of carelessness. As noted in the chapter, if figures are slightly off or facts could be interpreted multiple ways, a libel charge isn't likely to stick—the law requires negligence and/or reckless disregard for the truth. From the journalist's point of view this seems reasonable; but putting yourself in the position of a story subject, do you think it's fair? Ask your students: Should reporters who have a slippery relationship with truth deserve legal protection? Are minor inaccuracies inherent in the job? Are there nonlegal factors that should force journalists toward more accurate reporting?

3. In the age of social networking, some say privacy is a disappearing concept. Yet the right to privacy is an area of legal concern for journalists because many have been sued for invasion of privacy and related issues. Ask your students where we should draw the line in today's society. Is anything you've ever written online fair game, including email or other messages meant to be private? Does clicking "Post" or "Send" imply consent for any message to be public? How about material written and/or posted before turning 18?

Identification Questions

1. Intruding on people, physically or otherwise, is considered _____ if they are in a place where they have a reasonable expectation of privacy.

2. Perhaps the most serious breach of journalistic ethics is _____, the act of inventing false facts, interviews or other elements of news and reporting them as true.

3. _____ is the publication or airing in writing or pictures of false statements that expose someone to public hatred, contempt or ridicule.

4. A person whose reputation or person has been injured through the unlawful actions of another party may be awarded _____, financial compensation awarded by a court.

5. The U.S. Supreme Court has ruled that the First Amendment protects the publication of all "fair comment and criticism" about public figures unless the plaintiff can prove the statements were made with "actual _____."

6. Intentionally representing the words or ideas of someone else as your own is _____, a serious charge in both journalism and academia.

7. If a person gives _____ to be interviewed or photographed, publication of that material is not generally considered to be invasion of privacy.

8. At the heart of libel law is the conflict between two important interests: freedom of speech and the importance of _____.

9. Contrary to what Web surfers might believe, online _____, or posting hostile or insulting messages on the Internet, can carry the risk of libel suits.

10. Journalists can be charged with invasion of privacy for publishing a story that places people in a "_____," by printing or showing them acting in an inaccurate way that reasonable people could consider offensive.

ANSWERS: 1: TRESPASSING; 2: FABRICATION; 3: LIBEL; 4: DAMAGES; 5: MALICE; 6: PLAGIARISM; 7: CONSENT; 8: REPUTATION; 9: FLAMING; 10: FALSE LIGHT.

Web Links

- Libel & Privacy Invasion (Student Press Law Center):
  http://www.splc.org/knowyourrights/legalresearch.asp?maincat=4
- Tip Sheets: Ethics (Poynter):
  http://www.poynter.org/how-tos/10532/tip-sheets-ethics-1994-2010/
- Eight Simple Rules for Doing Accurate Journalism (*Columbia Journalism Review*):
  http://www.cjr.org/behind_the_news/eight_simple_rules_for_doing_a.php?page=all
- The 10 Commandments of News (John Maxwell Hamilton and George A. Krimsky):
  http://www.jmc.sjsu.edu/faculty/rcraig/10cmdmts.html
- Students offer new rules for accurate journalism (Poynter):
  http://www.poynter.org/latest-news/regret-the-error/160985/students-offer-new-rules-for-accurate-journalism/

(Note—if a link no longer works, search the title and source of the article to locate it online.)

CHAPTER 17
FIRST ASSIGNMENTS

Chapter Summary

Everyone who has been a professional journalist has a story about the drudgery of their first job. Maybe it didn't involve pouring coffee and sorting mail, but it almost certainly included taking the stories or beats nobody else wanted. Many of the best college reporters are sorely disappointed or bored with their first journalism job, but in this chapter, the authors aim to prepare students for such realities. They discuss the types of stories new reporters are commonly assigned, some of the techniques they should use and elements that every story should contain.

Discussion Topics

1. Talk about the realities of starting your first journalism job. If you have personal stories to share, this is a great time to do it. Fitting into any new work environment can be difficult, but new reporters often have to navigate the existing newsroom culture and fit in with colleagues who can be intimidating. Discuss not only the mundane tasks new reporters often perform—typing community events columns and calendars, putting together lists, covering small events etc.—but also how to work your way into better assignments. If students have completed internships, have them share their experiences as part of the discussion.

2. If you can, bring in a former student who now works in journalism to talk to students about what he/she had to overcome to succeed in the business. Students often respond very well to someone who was in their shoes not long ago. Have your former student talk for a few minutes, but leave lots of time for questions and answers. Ideally the former student will provide business cards or contact information for students who want to keep in touch. Usually only one or two will actually follow up on this, but it's a nice gesture that can help demystify the prospect of working in journalism, even for those who don't follow up.

3. Talk to the class about covering fire and police stories. Out of all the stories that young reporters may be assigned, these are often the most intense because of the nature of the events involved. Discuss the protocols and the order in which reporters must often gather information from witnesses and police/emergency personnel. If you have a campus police force, bringing in the chief or the public information officer to talk to the group is a good

idea—it can give students a sense of how these stories work, and if they end up working for campus media, they'll have already made an important connection.

In-Class Exercises

1. Have students attend a local city council meeting in your area, then write up a story about it in class the next day. Give them the assignment in advance so they can get up to speed on the issues, people and institutions involved. They'll make some mistakes, but this is great practice for a story they'll almost certainly be assigned early in their professional journalism careers.

2. Find some press releases for local community events in your area—preferably ones that vary in detail, quality of writing and significance of event. Present these to your students and have them write up how they would proceed in covering the event described. Would they immediately contact organizers and plan to attend? Would they get more information about the event and the people involved before deciding whether to cover it? Would they talk to their editors about whether it was really worth covering? Or would they simply ignore it and cover something else? Most important, why did they choose this action?

3. Using local media Web sites, locate some stories about fires in your area. If possible, these should include a mix of home or business fires and also brush fires and those in wilderness areas. Have your students read these and write up the similarities and differences between them. Are there common themes across all of the stories, or are fires in populated areas covered dramatically differently? Are fire personnel quoted in every story? How are different types of fires discussed in terms of severity—by acres burned, property damaged, estimated costs or what?

Identification Questions

1. A common early assignment is covering a _____ by a local newsmaker.

2. As a new reporter, you'll likely be inundated with news _____ from people who want you to cover their events, products or activities.

3. Community events such as fairs, _____ and craft shows are popular with readers and often important to the community.

4. The people's right to know is protected by state and federal laws known as open meeting or "_____" laws.

5. As a young reporter, show some _____—don't be afraid to admit you're new and still learning.

6. In traffic or elsewhere, news organizations seldom cover _____ unless they cause fatalities, significant property damage or involve a prominent person.

7. Young reporters are often asked to cover lots of _____, whether they involve city councils, school boards, planning commissions or other groups.

8. Items like names, ages, figures and time/place of the interview are referred to as "non-negotiable _____"—elements that every story must contain to satisfy readers, viewers and listeners.

9. When covering police or _____ stories, have respect for the people doing their jobs at the scene of the event.

10. Rather than covering meetings or community events by listing everything that happened, _____ the story by focusing on the people involved.

ANSWERS: 1: SPEECH; 2: RELEASES; 3: FESTIVALS; 4: SUNSHINE; 5: HUMILITY; 6: ACCIDENTS; 7: MEETINGS; 8: NECESSITIES; 9: FIRE; 10: HUMANIZE.

Web Links

- Making the most of meetings (NewsLab):
  http://www.newslab.org/strategies/meetings.htm
- How To Cover Speeches (CubReporters.org):
  http://journalism-education.cubreporters.org/2010/08/how-to-cover-speeches.html
- First Draft: Young Reporters (Society of Professional Journalists):
  http://blogs.spjnetwork.org/genj/tag/young-reporters/
- 5 ways young journalists can stay motivated, thrive in the newsroom (Tom Huang, Poynter):
  http://www.poynter.org/how-tos/career-development/170328/5-ways-young-journalists-can-stay-motivated-thrive-in-the-newsroom/
- Advice for Young Journalists (Anderson Cooper):
  http://www.andersoncooper.com/2011/11/18/whats-your-advice-for-young-journalists-audience-q-and-a/

(Note—if a link no longer works, search the title and source of the article to locate it online.)

CHAPTER 18
BEATS:
POLICE, COURTS, SPORTS, BUSINESS, EDUCATION AND MORE

Chapter Summary

It's rare that a journalism student will enter your class having already regularly covered a beat. Students tend to understand the concept of beats better than the reality, so this chapter is an opportunity to introduce them to what beat reporting is really like. If you can convey to your students the day-to-day nature of being the reporter in charge of a particular area or subject—with its burdens and opportunities—you'll have done them a huge favor. In this chapter, the authors cover common beats and the best ways to approach the job of regularly monitoring important institutions and people.

Discussion Topics

1. On every beat, persistence pays off. Discuss the nature of daily beat reporting, of how checking in with people regularly can make you part of a community and lead to stories that no other reporter can get. Ask students who they think a beat reporter covering your local community should talk to regularly to stay on top of events. Feel free to chime in with your own suggestions. Also, discuss the process of cultivating sources—what's appropriate and what's too much?

2. The section in the chapter on real estate reporter Harold Bubil is an interesting example of a beat reporter "building a brand"—of becoming the go-to local expert on his area of expertise. Talk to your students about the idea of brand building in the digital age—many successful reporters have used their own knowledge of a particular subject to make themselves into known commodities online beyond their news outlet's coverage area.

3. Introduce your students to the story of Sara Ganim, a young reporter who parlayed a seemingly unremarkable court reporting job into a Pulitzer Prize at age 24. By simply following up on leads and remaining vigilant about pursuing a story for many months while continuing to work on other assignments, she uncovered evidence that a former Penn State University football coach had sexually abused children. On one hand, not every beat reporter will find a story like this; but on the other hand, she recognized the

potential magnitude of this story and didn't let it go in spite of some leads that went nowhere. There's plenty of material about Ganim and this case available online.

4. Bring in a local beat reporter to talk to your students. Whether the reporter is covering police, courts, the city council or another beat, the chance for students to meet and speak with someone who does this every day is invaluable. If you don't know anyone who fits this description, just look in your local media for bylines of people covering stories in your area. Reporters are generally happy to accommodate journalism classes—many of them attended journalism school and enjoy actually being the ones to answer questions for a change.

In-Class Exercises

1. Take your class on a trip to the local courthouse. If your school is in a small town, you might want to take students to a city nearby and visit a courthouse there—larger cities generally have more going on, and you'll get more variety (not just lots of traffic tickets). Call the courthouse and see if there's a contact for reporters—if so, arrange the visit through that person. Ideally he/she can discuss the information available through public records and provide examples for them to examine.

2. Introduce a scenario for your students. They've just gotten a job with a local media outlet in your area (you can pick a specific one if you like). They are to cover a region that comprises three suburbs and an incorporated area (again, picking specific communities in your area would help). Given them 30 minutes to go online and compile a list of people they should contact and meet with in that area. Ask for names, occupations, office addresses and phone numbers, email addresses and anything else the student can put together.

3. Students fresh out of school are seldom put on the police beat immediately. In student media, however, they might well get that job right away. Locate some good examples of police reporting from your local media outlets and present them to your students. Have them look for common features and sources across all the articles. Whereas the crimes may be different, are there elements they can identify to help them understand the structure of most police reporting? Do the examples illustrate questions that should always be asked or issues common to these stories?

Identification Questions

1. Because beginning reporters tend to be young, have no children and own no property, the _____ beat is usually the one they are least prepared to cover.

2. Beat reporters can use property, court and police records in their work but should always make _____ the foundation of their reporting.

3. Journalists who've shown outstanding work on basic beats, or those with education or professional practice in the field, will sometimes be assigned a _____ beat, considered a prestigious assignment.

4. Each beat is a _____, a sphere of knowledge, skills, rules and language that the reporter must master to translate what's happening for news consumers.

5. A "_____ tour" involves physically getting out into the community you're covering, talking to people, visiting businesses and getting acquainted with how it works.

6. Beat reporters sometimes need to translate their beat's _____ and vocabulary, using words that readers will understand to explain events and activities.

7. Traditionally, the inner city has been the center of news, but these days _____ also generate their fair share of newsworthy events.

8. It's vitally important that beat reporters stay _____, to keep on top of everything going on within the community they cover.

9. Beat reporters need to _____ sources, keeping in touch with them regularly to see if they have any new information.

10. The _____ beat is often described as a feast-or-famine job—it can involve listening to a scanner for hours, then suddenly you can be in the middle of a major story.

ANSWERS: 1: GOVERNMENT; 2: PEOPLE; 3: SPECIALTY; 4: DOMAIN; 5: SHOE LEATHER; 6: JARGON; 7: SUBURBS; 8: ORGANIZED; 9: CULTIVATE; 10: POLICE.

Web Links

- Good Examples of Beat Reporting (The Vagabond Journalist): http://d4n12i.wordpress.com/2008/09/23/good-examples-of-beat-reporting/
- Beat Reporting (Poynter): http://www.newsu.org/resources/training-tips/163
- Five lessons from deep beat reporting (Online News Association): http://journalists.org/2012/05/22/five-lessons-from-deep-beat-reporting/
- The Crime Beat: Crime Reporting (Dave Krajicek, Criminal Justice Journalists): http://www.justicejournalism.org/crimeguide/chapter01/sidebars/chap01_xside1.html
- On the Beat: Covering Cops and Crime (NewsU): http://www.newsu.org/courses/beat-covering-cops-and-crime

(Note—if a link no longer works, search the title and source of the article to locate it online.)

CHAPTER 19
OBITUARIES

Chapter Summary

There is scarcely any subject beginning reporters are more uncomfortable with than obituaries. Most of them are young and may never have had to deal with the death of anyone close to them. Still, it's not uncommon for obits to be among the first assignments for a young writer. A good way for students to understand obits is as little biographies of a person's life. With today's digital technologies, they can have all kinds of dimensions beyond text stories. In this chapter, the authors guide young reporters on how to approach the task and fill them in on the customs, challenges and expectations that come with the territory.

Discussion Topics

1. In the news business, there's an important distinction drawn between obituaries written by journalists and those paid for by loved ones. The former is what this chapter is about, while the latter are considered basically advertising. Accordingly, they're generally set aside in their own section and labeled as paid obits; and because they're written by loved ones, they tend to be much more effusive and flowery than anything else that appears in the paper. Tell the group about this difference, and point out that some journalists dislike having this type of writing alongside actual journalism. Ask the students if this troubles them or whether the circumstances involved excuse the overwrought prose.

2. It's noted in the chapter that obits tend to follow a fairly rigid structure but that there are exceptions. Find some examples of local obits and show the students how they're organized and written. Do the ones about well-known local people have different characteristics than others?

3. In the last couple of decades, the "appreciation" format has become widely adopted in obituaries for celebrities, politicians and even some local newsmakers. The format— sometimes called a "Style Appreciation" because it was brought to popularity by the *Washington Post*'s Style section—has its share of critics because it tends to omit the normal inclusion of parents and other family members. It's also criticized as a "whitewash" because it seldom deals with any adversity in the decedent's life. Have your students read some examples of this format and discuss whether it is an acceptable substitute for a standard obit or whether more details would be preferable. Also discuss

the notion that because it's usually reserved for celebrities or other success stories, it's a subtle put-down of working classes. Do they believe this is true?

In-Class Exercises

1. As noted in the chapter, writing advance obits is common practice at national news outlets. With this in mind, select three to five public figures and assign them numbers as well as dates and causes of death. Then have your students number off accordingly and have them use online resources to write a feature obit for the person corresponding with their number. In addition to writing the obit, tell them to make sure to list URLs of the sources of their information at the end. The obits should follow the guidelines listed in the chapter.

2. The discussion of including both good and bad in obits is especially tricky when the subject of the obit is a celebrity or political figure. When U.S. Senator Ted Kennedy died in August of 2009, he'd served in the Senate for more than 40 years and was lauded by many for his efforts enacting legislation in areas across the political spectrum. What was left out of some obits was his most notorious incident—the 1969 auto accident at Chappaquiddick Island, MA, that took the life of his passenger, Mary Jo Kopechne. Look online and find some sample Kennedy obits—if possible, find some that note the accident and some that don't. Introduce these facts to your students, show them the obits and have them write up an explanation of whether they believe omitting the incident from obits was acceptable under the circumstances. Why or why not, and how does this decision relate to some of the concepts in the book?

3. In the book, the authors discuss the "common man" feature obit, written in feature style even if the subject wasn't famous. Locate some examples of these, have the students read them and then see if they can find common themes and structures among them. Are there certain storytelling styles and devices used, regardless of the backgrounds of the people involved? Is the format as rigid as that of news obits? Does it serve a different purpose than the news obit, and is there material missing in the "common man" format that might have been included in a traditional obit?

Identification Questions

1. Because family members pay close attention to what appears in obituaries, they tend to require more _____ after publication than any other type of story.

2. In the wake of the terrorist attacks of Sept. 11, 2001, rather than running full obituaries for all of those who were killed, the *New York Times* won praise for running brief _____ of the victims.

3. An obituary fleshed out with detailed biographical information, including anecdotes, descriptions, quotes and reminiscences, is called a _____ obit.

4. Taboos—things not to be mentioned—in obituaries over the years have included _____, which faded as cancer became better understood but reappeared with the AIDS epidemic of the 1980s.

5. More than most types of news stories, obituaries adhere to a formulaic _____, though this can differ with the deaths of prominent individuals.

6. An _____ is an essay that explores the impact of a person's life—and death— often written by someone familiar with the person or the person's work.

7. A well-written obituary is one that finds a strong _____, the central thread that captures a person's essence.

8. The report of a death that is considered noteworthy because of the prominence of the individual or his or her place in the community is known as a _____ obit.

9. Journalists writing obits face special pressures when the cause of death is _____ for fear of inspiring copycats or upsetting the family.

10. _____ obits have made it easy to create a tribute that can be viewed and contributed to by friends and family

ANSWERS: 1: CORRECTIONS; 2: PROFILES; 3: FEATURE; 4: DISEASE; 5: STRUCTURE; 6: APPRECIATION; 7: FOCUS; 8: NEWS; 9: SUICIDE; 10: ONLINE.

Web Links

- The Art of Obituary Writing (NPR):
  http://www.npr.org/templates/story/story.php?storyId=1079988
- Society of Professional Obituary Writers:
  http://obitwriters.org/
- Jobless journalists could find a business model in obituaries (Steve Buttry):
  http://stevebuttry.wordpress.com/2010/07/16/jobless-journalists-could-find-a-business-model-in-obituaries/
- On the Beat: Writing Obituaries (NewsU):
  http://www.newsu.org/courses/beat-writing-obituaries
- Case of mistaken identity stuns families (Theodore Kim, *USA Today*):
  http://www.usatoday.com/news/nation/2006-05-31-indiana-mistaken-identity_x.htm

(Note—if a link no longer works, search the title and source of the article to locate it online.)

CHAPTER 20
EMERGENCIES, DISASTERS AND CONFLICTS: FROM WEATHER TO WAR

Chapter Summary

Disasters are acknowledged as the hardest type of story to prepare for, thanks to their unpredictability and the fact that every one is different. Because of their unpredictability, they're also something that beginning journalists might be called on to cover. If there's any way to prepare students for such events, it's to present scenarios that make students think about all the specifics that make it hard to get information from victims or officials. In this chapter, the authors discuss the challenges inherent in all kinds of emergencies and show young reporters how to approach them safely and effectively.

Discussion Topics

1. The commitment by news organizations to report the news under any circumstances was illustrated vividly by the staff of the New Orleans *Times-Picayune* in the wake of Hurricane Katrina in 2005. Operating out of private homes and cars, using the reporters' own computers, the *Times-Picayune* continued publishing electronic editions of its newspaper while its presses were unavailable. These efforts kept the local community and wider online audience informed and won the *Times-Picayune* a Pulitzer Prize. Discuss how these efforts reflect the culture of journalism in times of crisis and disaster.

2. Whether it's covering wars, earthquakes or terrorist attacks, lots of journalists want to be where the action is. However, the truth is that you can't cover anything if you're killed or seriously injured in the process. The Dart Center for Journalism and Trauma, a project of the Columbia University Graduate School of Journalism, has put together a list of "Five Steps to Covering a Disaster Effectively," which is available on the Dart Center Web site. Go through these with your students and discuss how they might apply to covering recent disasters with which they're familiar.

3. The tsunamis that struck Asia in 2004 and 2011 captured the world's attention, killing thousands and leaving more than one million homeless. Some of the most dramatic news coverage of these catastrophes involved home video, whether shared on television networks or online at platforms such as YouTube and Vimeo. Discuss the role of user-submitted content in disaster coverage today. Is anyone with a camera a journalist, or can their footage instead become a part of a journalistic report? You might contrast today's

culture of freely sharing footage with the case of Abraham Zapruder, who shot the infamous home movie footage of President Kennedy's assassination. Zapruder was paid $150,000 by Life magazine for rights to the film in 1963, which equates to more than $1 million in today's money.

4. Although people are generally thankful for reporters covering their stories in the wake of disasters, that support can disappear if writers also discover wrongdoing among rescuers or government agencies. The reporters who follow the angle of "What went wrong?" are often vilified and accused of taking advantage of a tragedy. Discuss the dynamics that can emerge from such a situation and what journalists need to do to avoid such accusations.

In-Class Exercises

1. Disaster and emergency coverage has changed dramatically with the coming of cell phones and other technologies that allow real-time coverage from the scene of an event. With Twitter, journalists can get updates out immediately from wherever they are covering a story. Having said this, tweets have not always proven to be reliable news sources, even when written by journalists at the scene of an event. In their haste to be first, sometimes mistakes are made that might not have been released to the public in previous generations (as in the Sago mine disaster mentioned in the book). Ask your students to write up a discussion of the pros and cons of using Twitter, blogs and other means of instant updating while covering a story as a professional journalist. Everyone wants to be first, but would you want to endanger your livelihood and journalistic reputation by publishing bad information on the fly?

2. The book notes that as soon as *The Washington Post* received word of a gunman on the Virginia Tech campus in April 2007, the *Post*'s print and online staffs began formulating a coverage plan. This involved use of multiple staff members in the newsroom and on the scene providing different kinds of content and updating it regularly. Introduce this concept to your students, then present this scenario. You're an editor at the *Denver Post* in July 2012, and you've just received word about shootings in a movie theater in suburban Aurora. Knowing only this, and with the knowledge of news staffs from previous chapters, have the students assemble a coverage plan for providing full coverage for both the paper's Web site and print product.

3. In the chapter, the authors discuss the dilemma of journalists who cover wars while traveling with military units. On one hand, this gives reporters an unprecedented look at the challenges faced by soldiers and the devastation of war. On the other hand, it can put reporters in harm's way, with the soldiers surrounding them serving as their only line of

defense. Some critics have argued that the situation poses a different threat—to the journalist's ability to be critical. As many previous wars have shown, soldiers and their leaders don't always behave admirably, and the reporter's role has traditionally been to remain as objective as possible in reporting the truth. But is it realistic to expect reporters to be critical of soldiers and officers whom they've befriended and who are expected to defend his life? Or is this whole arrangement ethically questionable and perhaps not worth the trouble? Introduce this dilemma to your students and have them write up their responses, being sure to explain why they believe what they do.

Identification Questions

1. Police officers, firefighters, paramedics and other rescue personnel are called "_____" because they descend on disaster scenes immediately.

2. One way to convey suspense and drama in a disaster story is with a "_____," or chronological narrative.

3. The media's _____ role sometimes upsets people in the wake of disasters, but they can reveal abuses and mismanagement that the public should know about.

4. A _____ is an online tool that shows the public exactly where a disaster occurred.

5. During wartime, _____ journalists travel with military units to uncover the full truth of what happens during battles.

6. The need to _____ and attribute should be a reporter's mantra, especially when an emergency strikes and rumors, speculation and misinformation fly.

7. If you're the only reporter on the scene of an emergency, your role may be to send in "_____"—raw data or brief passages—to a reporter who will use them to write the main story.

8. Always important in reporting, specific _____ are especially vital in disaster scenarios because they enable readers to envision the event.

9. A hybrid of old and new, the breaking news _____ combines online real-time updates with the inverted pyramid to quickly report breaking news.

10. Whether online or in print, a visual _____ of the events surrounding a disaster help the public understand what happened by identifying pivotal moments.

ANSWERS: 1: FIRST RESPONDERS; 2: TICK-TOCK; 3: WATCHDOG; 4: LOCATOR MAP; 5: EMBEDDED; 6: VERIFY; 7: FEEDS; 8: DETAILS; 9:BLOG; 10: TIMELINE.

Web Links

- Five Steps to Covering a Disaster Effectively (Dart Center): http://dartcenter.org/content/five-steps-to-covering-disaster-effectively
- Disaster coverage (Poynter): http://www.poynter.org/tag/disaster-coverage/
- *Roanoke Times* live blog of Virginia Tech shootings: http://www.roanoke.com/news/nrv/breaking/wb/113294
- Journalist Security Guide (Committee to Protect Journalists): http://cpj.org/reports/2012/04/journalist-security-guide.php
- 10 Media Lessons of Gulf Disaster Coverage (Radio-Television Digital News Association): http://www.rtdna.org/pages/posts/10-media-lessons-of-gulf-disaster-coverage1466.php

(Note—if a link no longer works, search the title and source of the article to locate it online.)

CHAPTER 21
GETTING AND KEEPING A JOB

Chapter Summary

In recent years, all journalism students have heard is that the job market is impossible. Perhaps because of this, many have developed a fatalistic attitude about getting hired while others simply worry. Yet the best journalism students do continue to get jobs in the industry. Instructors have the task of not only preparing students to work as journalists but also to overcome their fears and enter the job market. In this chapter, the authors provide some advice for putting together a portfolio of work and succeeding in a competitive marketplace.

Discussion Topics

1. Bring in a top editor from a local news outlet to talk to students about jobs and internships. Reading about how to prepare for the job market is one thing, but getting a chance to speak with someone who has been in on hiring decisions has a far more immediate impact. Have the editor discuss everything from what students should do while in school to preparing portfolios, résumés and cover letters.

2. Introduce students to JournalismJobs.com and go through some job listings with the group. Discuss the nature of the jobs listed—are some types of jobs more common than others? Are some areas of the country hiring more and others hiring less? Ask the students what they can learn by looking through these listings.

3. Ask colleagues for examples of résumés and cover letters or find some online. Go through these point by point with your students and discuss how different ones are formatted and the information they contain. A useful point to make is that not all successful résumés or cover letters are the same—they simply have to be effective at promoting an individual job seeker on his/her own terms.

4. If you have students who have completed journalism internships in your class, ask them to talk about their experiences in the workplace. Make sure they talk not only about the tasks they performed in the newsroom but also what they saw others doing. Were reporters always on the phone talking to sources, always online doing research or outside the newsroom?

In-Class Exercises

1. Find some examples of résumés and cover letters online. Present these to your students, and have them write up a summary of which ones are effective and which are ineffective and why. Stress to them that it's not about how much experience someone lists but rather how effectively that experience is conveyed. Also have them be on the lookout for padding of résumés—trying to make items look more impressive than they are.

2. Prepare a journalism job listing or identify one on a Web site. Give students a homework assignment to prepare a portfolio containing a résumé, cover letter and clips for this listing and bring it to the next class. Then break the class up into groups of two or three and have them critique each other's portfolios face to face. Students can learn a lot from this sort of activity, both about their own portfolios and others.

3. Locate some examples of interactive résumés online and show them to your students. Ask the students whether the addition of links and multimedia content make these more impressive than standard documents or whether they add more style than substance. Also be sure to ask whether interactive résumés are more effective for visual journalists (photographers, videographers, designers etc.) than for reporters or whether they offer different kinds of advantages for writers.

Identification Questions

1. A _____ letter is written directly to the person doing the hiring for a position, and should be tailored specifically to the job in question.

2. Every journalism major should prepare a _____ of their best work, whether articles, photos or video, to use when looking for a job.

3. Regardless of whether you're in print, broadcast or online journalism, a good piece of advice is to start at a _____ local publication where you'll get plenty of opportunities.

4. Bring a _____ to job interviews, to take notes during the interview, on what you see in the newsroom and anything else that might tell you about the job.

5. An online _____ allows you to include links to your work and email it to potential employers rather than just listing your accomplishments on paper.

6. Having a good _____ is important—if you're willing to be plugged in to do what the organization needs, you'll become a valuable employee.

7. Employers are usually interested if you've completed an _____, since it shows you've had some professional experience before graduation.

8. The best _____ are people who are familiar with your work, such as professional supervisors or journalism professors with whom you've worked closely.

9. Samples of your work are generally known as "_____," whether they're actually cut from a newspaper or printouts of online content.

10. News organizations want to know you are proficient with _____ software such as Photoshop, Flash or Final Cut Pro.

ANSWERS: 1: COVER; 2: PORTFOLIO; 3: SMALL; 4: NOTEBOOK; 5: RÉSUMÉ; 6: ATTITUDE; 7: INTERNSHIP; 8: REFERENCES; 9: CLIPS; 10: MULTIMEDIA.

Web Links

- Journalism Jobs:
  http://www.journalismjobs.com
- Good First Journalism Jobs (CubReporters.org):
  http://cubreporters.org/jobs.html
- More journalism majors finding jobs after graduation (Steve Myers, Poynter):
  http://www.poynter.org/latest-news/mediawire/184607/more-journalism-majors-finding-jobs-after-graduation/
- Create a Great Resume for Journalism Jobs (Suite 101):
  http://suite101.com/article/create-a-great-resume-for-journalism-jobs-a199634

(Note—if a link no longer works, search the title and source of the article to locate it online.)

CPSIA information can be obtained at www.ICGtesting.com
Printed in the USA
BVOW050334270613

324449BV00005B/12/P